2000 THINGS YOU SHOULD KNOW

First published in 2000 by
Miles Kelly Publishing Ltd
Bardfield Centre, Great Bardfield, Essex, CM7 4SL

2 4 6 8 10 9 7 5 3 1

Project Manager: Ian Paulyn
Art Director: Clare Sleven
Editorial Director: Paula Borton
Production: Rachel Jones
Artwork Commissioning: Janice Bracken
Assistants: Lesley Cartlidge, Liberty Newton
Indexer: Jane Parker
Written and designed by Barnsbury Books

British Library Cataloguing-in-Publication Data
A catalogue record for this book is available from the British library

ISBN 1-902947-79-7

Contact us by e-mail: info@mileskelly.net

Printed in Hong Kong

WORLD HISTORY

2000 THINGS YOU
SHOULD KNOW

John Farndon

Miles KELLY

PUBLISHING

Contents

ANCIENT HISTORY 8-63

Contents

MODERN HISTORY 66-121

1000
THINGS
YOU SHOULD KNOW ABOUT

ANCIENT
HISTORY

KEY

The Americas and Pacific

Classical World

Europe

Africa and the Near East

Asia and the Far East

People and lifestyles

Search for the past

Origins of mankind

▼ *Experts once thought humans evolved in a single line from australopiths, through Homo habilis (1), Homo erectus (2) and Neanderthal man (3) to humans (4). They now realize there were many branches.*

- **Humans and apes** have so many similarities – such as long arms and fingers, and a big brain – most experts think they must have evolved from the same creature.

- **The common ancestor** may be four-legged orang-utan-like creatures called dryopithecines that lived in trees 22-10 million years ago (mya), like 'Proconsul' from E. Africa.

- **The break came when** 'hominids' (human-like apes) began to live on the ground and walk on two legs.

- **Footprints** of three bipedal (two-legged) creatures from 4 mya were found preserved in ash at Laetoli, Tanzania.

- **The oldest hominid** is called *Ardipithecus ramidus*, known from 4.4 mya bone fragments found in Aramis, Ethiopia.

- **Many very early** hominids are australopiths ('southern apes'), like the *Australopithecus anamensis* from 4.2 mya.

- **Australopiths** were only 1 m tall and their brain was about the same size as an ape's, but they were bipedal.

- **The best known** australopith is 'Lucy', a skeleton of *Australopithecus afarensis* of 3 mya, found in Kenya in 1974.

- **Lucy's discoverers** Don Johanson and Maurice Tieb called her Lucy because they were listening to the Beatles song 'Lucy in the Sky with Diamonds' at the time.

- **Many early hominid** remains are just skulls. Lucy was an almost complete skeleton. She showed that hominids learned to walk upright before their brains got bigger.

Handy Man

- **2.5-1.8 million years ago** the first really human-like hominids appeared. These hominids are all given the genus (group) name *Homo*, and include us.

- **The best known** early Homos are *Homo rudolfensis* and *Homo habilis*.

- **The first Homos** were taller than australopiths and had bigger brains.

- **Unlike australopiths,** Homos ate meat. They may have been forced to eat meat by a drying of the climate that cut the amount of plant food available.

- **Brains need** a lot of food, and eating meat gave the extra nourishment needed for bigger brains.

▶ *Skulls show that the first Homos, like Homo habilis, had brains of 650 cubic cm (cc) – twice as big as australopiths. Ours are about 1,400 cc. But they had ape-like faces with protruding jaws and sloping foreheads.*

- **Homo habilis** is known from bits of hand bones, a jaw and a skull found in Tanzania's Olduvai Gorge in 1961.

- **Homo habilis** means Handy Man. He gets his name because he has a good grip for wielding tools – with a thumb that can be rotated to meet the tip of a finger. This is called an 'opposable thumb'.

- **The first Homos** used bones or stones to break open bones to get at the marrow. Later they sharpened stones to cut meat for eating and hides for clothing. They may have even built simple shelters to live in.

- **Some experts** think the bulge in 'Broca's area' of some *Homo habilis* skulls suggests they could speak in a crude way. Most think they could not.

- **The first Homos** lived for a million or more years alongside 'robust' (bigger) australopiths, such as *Paranthropus boisei*.

Man the hunter

- **About 2 mya,** a much taller Homo called *Homo ergaster* appeared. Ergasters were the first creatures to have bodies much like ours, with long legs and straight backs.

- **Adult ergasters** were 1.6 m tall, weighed 65 kg and had brains of 850 cubic cm, well over half as big as ours.

- **Ergasters** did not just scavenge for meat like *Homo habilis*. They went hunting for large animals.

- **To hunt** and cut up meat, ergaster-shaped stones, chipping flakes off to make proper double-edge blades or 'hand-axes'. Experts call this Acheulean tool-making.

- **To hunt,** ergasters had to work together, so co-operation was the key to their success – and may have quickly led to the development of speech.

- **Ergasters** may have painted their bodies with red ochre.

> ★ STAR FACT ★
> Long legs and working together helped ergaster spread beyond Africa into Asia and maybe Europe.

▲ *Human development began when hominids learned to hunt together.*

- **Shortly after** ergaster came *Homo erectus* (Upright Man).

- **Erectus** remains are found as far from Africa as Java. 700,000 year-old stone tools on the Indonesian island of Flores suggest they may have travelled by boat.

- **Erectus** learned to light fires, so they could live in colder places, and make a wider range of food edible by cooking.

Neanderthals and others

- **Hominids** appeared in Europe much later. The oldest, called *Homo antecessor*, dates from 800,000 years ago. This may have been a kind of erectus, or another species.

- **800-600,000 years ago** *Homo Heidelbergensis* appeared in Europe, Asia and Africa.

- **Heidelbergensis** may be a single species that came from Africa – or various species that evolved in different places.

- **Heidelbergensis** has many features in common with erectus, but is a major step on the way to modern humans with, for the first time, a brain as big as ours.

▶ *Most early hominid remains have been found in Africa. Many species – including modern humans – may have emerged first in Africa, then migrated elsewhere. These are sites where remains were found.*

- **Heidelbergensis** made good stone tools by making the core first, then shaping the blade with a single blow.

- **Heidelbergensis** was ancestor to Neanderthal Man, who lived in Europe from 250,000 to 30,000 years ago.

- **Neanderthals** were named after the Neander valley in Germany, where remains were found in 1856.

- **Neanderthals** were slightly shorter than modern humans but much stronger and with bigger brains. They must have been formidable hunters.

- **Neanderthals** buried their dead, often with tributes of flowers.

- **Neanderthals** lived in Croatia 28,000 years ago – long after modern humans. No one knows why they died out, leaving humans alone.

Swanscombe
Boxgrove
Cro-Magnon
Grimaldi
Dolní Vestonice
Vindija, Croatia
Dmanisi
Shanidar
Skhul
Tabun
Bahr el Ghazal
Omo
Hadar (Lucy)
Nariokotome
Olduvai
Laetoli
Kabwe
Sterkfontein
Taung
Swartkrans
Klasies River

✤ Australopith, 1-4 mya
✤ H. habilis, 2.5-1 mya
✤ H. ergaster, 2 0.5 mya
✤ H. H'berg, 500-100,000 yrs
✤ N'thal 250-30,000 yrs
✤ H. sapiens 30,000 yrs

Modern humans

- **The scientific name** for modern humans is *Homo Sapiens Sapiens*. The word *Sapiens* is used twice to distinguish us from *Homo Sapiens Neanderthalis* (Neanderthal Man).

- **Unlike Neanderthals,** modern humans have a prominent chin and a flat face with a high forehead.

- **Some scientists** think the similarity of DNA in our bodies means all humans are descended from a woman nicknamed 'Eve', who they calculate lived in Africa about 200,000 years ago. DNA is the special molecule in every body-cell that carries the body's instructions for life.

- **The oldest human skulls** are 130,000 years old and were found in the Omo Basin in Ethiopia and the Klasies river in South Africa.

- **About 100,000 years ago** modern humans began to spread out into Eurasia from Africa.

- **The earliest modern Europeans** are called Cro-Magnon Man, after the caves in France's Dordogne valley where skeletons from 35,000 years ago were found in 1868.

- **Modern humans** reached Australia by boat from Indonesia 50,000 years ago. They reached the Americas from Asia about the same time.

- **Modern humans** lived alongside Neanderthals for tens of thousands of years in the Middle East and Europe.

- **Modern humans** were probably the first creatures to speak what we would call language. Some scientists think language was a sudden genetic accident which gave humans a huge advantage.

- **With modern humans** came rapid advances in stone-tool technology, the building of wooden huts, a rise in population and a growing interest in art.

◀ *Both modern humans and Neanderthals used beautifully made spears for hunting.*

Cave painters

- **Prehistoric people** sometimes lived in caves, but more often they went into caves to paint and draw.

- **The world's** most famous cave paintings, at Lascaux in France and Altamira in Spain, were found by children.

- **Carbon dating** shows the paintings in Lascaux are 31,000 years old. Those in Chauvet in the French Ardèche are nearly twice as old.

- **The pictures** at Cougnac in France were painted over a period of 10,000 years.

- **Most paintings** in caves show large animals such as bison, deer, horses and mammoths.

- **Caves** may have been the temples of prehistoric times, and the paintings linked to religious rituals.

- **Cave artists** often painted by spitting paint, just as Australian aboriginals do today.

- **To reach** the 14,000-year-old paintings in France's Pergouset, you must crawl through 150 m of passages.

- **In the caves** at Nerja in Spain there are rock formations that prehistoric people played like a xylophone.

- **The aboriginal paintings** on rocks in Arnhemland, Northern Territory, Australia may be over 50,000 years old.

◀ *The most famous cave paintings are those in the Hall of Bulls at Lascaux in France. These paintings show bison.*

The Stone Ages

- **The Stone Ages** were the ages before humans discovered metals and so used mainly stones for making tools.

- **Stone tools** were made by chipping away stones to make hammers, spear and arrow heads, knives and scrapers.

- **People usually** used local stone, but sometimes good stones were imported from long distances.

- **Early Europeans** used mainly flint. Africans used quartz, chert, basalt and obsidian.

- **In Europe** there were three Stone Ages : Old (Palaeolithic), Middle (Mesolithic) and New (Neolithic).

▶ *Mesolithic people hunted with bows and arrows and flint-tipped spears.*

- **The Palaeolithic** began 2 million years ago when various human ancestors gathered plants and hunted with stone weapons.

- **The Mesolithic** was the transition from the Old to the New Stone Age – after the Last Ice Age ended around 12,000 years ago.

- **The Neolithic** was the time when people began to settle down and farm. This occurred first in the Near East, about 10,000 years ago.

- **In 1981,** a pebble shaped into a female form, half a million years old was found at Berekhat Ram in Israel's Golan Heights.

- **Venus figurines** are plump stone female figures from c.25,000 years ago, found in Europe, e.g. the Czech Republic.

The Bronze Age

- **The Bronze Age** is the period of prehistory when people first began to use the metal bronze.

- **Bronze** is an alloy (mix) of copper with about 10% tin.

- **The first metals used** were probably lumps of pure gold and copper, beaten into shape to make ornaments in Turkey and Iran about 6000BC.

- **Metal ores** (metals mixed with other minerals) were probably discovered when certain stones were found to melt when heated in a kiln.

- **Around 4000BC,** metal smiths in southeast Europe and Iran began making copper axeheads with a central hole to take a wooden shaft.

- **The Copper Age** is the period when people used copper before they learned to alloy it with tin to make bronze. Metalworking with copper was flourishing in the early cities of Mesopotamia, in the Middle East, about 3500BC.

- **The Bronze Age** began several times between 3500 and 3000BC in the Near East, Balkans and

SE Asia when smiths discovered that, by adding a small quantity of tin, they could make bronze. Bronze is harder than copper and easier to make into a sharp blade.

- **Knowledge of bronze** spread slowly across Eurasia, but by 1500BC it was in use all the way from Europe to India.

- **The rarity of tin** spurred long-distance trade links – and the first mines, like the tin mines in Cornwall, England.

- **Bronze** can be cast – shaped by melting it into a clay mould (itself shaped with a wax model). For the first time people could make things any shape they wanted. Skilled smiths across Eurasia began to cast bronze to make everything from weapons to cooking utensils – and safety pins for clothes.

◀ *By 1000BC, beautiful metal swords and other weapons with sharp blades like this were being made all over Europe and western Asia.*

The Iron Age

▶ Maiden Castle in Dorset is the largest of around 1,000 hillforts built in southern Britain in the Iron Age. This is how it might have looked in about 300BC.

Typical Iron Age round houses, built of wood, and straw thatch

The hilltop village within the defences covered about 17 hectares

The inner rampart was 14 m high and topped by a fence of huge, upright timbers. It was faced with big limestone blocks, not grass

A series of ditches and banks were built up from clay

The entrance wound between ramparts to make life hard for attackers

The entrance through the inner ramparts had massive timber gates

▶ The cheapness and availability of iron in the Iron Age meant that even quite a poor man might have his own sword.

- **The Iron Age** is the time in prehistory when iron replaced bronze as the main metal.

- **The use of iron** was discovered by the Hittites in Anatolia, Turkey between 1500 and 1200BC. This discovery helped to make the Hittites immensely powerful for a few centuries.

- **Around 1200BC,** the Hittite Empire collapsed and the use of iron spread through Asia and central Europe. The Dorian Greeks became famous iron masters.

- **Tin is rare**, so bronze objects were made mostly for chieftains. Iron ore is common, so ordinary people could have metal objects such as cooking utensils.

- **Many ordinary farmers** could afford iron scythes and axes. With tough metal tools to clear fields and harvest crops quickly, farming developed much more rapidly.

- **Growth in population** put pressure on resources and warfare increased across Eurasia. Partly as a result, many northern Europe settlements developed into hillforts – hilltop sites protected by earth ramparts, ditches and stockades.

- **Around 650BC,** peoples skilled in iron working called Celts began to dominate northern Europe.

- **Iron working** reached China around 600BC. The Chinese used large bellows to boost furnace temperatures enough to melt ore in large quantities.

- **Iron tools** appearing in West Africa around 400BC were the basis of the Nok culture. Nok farmers speaking Bantu spread south and east all over Africa.

★ **STAR FACT** ★
In 1950, an Iron Age man was found in a peatbog at Tollund in Jutland, Denmark, perfectly preserved over 2,000 years.

Megaliths

- **Megalith** means 'giant stone'.
- **Megaliths** are monuments such as tombs made from huge blocks of stone, built in western Europe in the Neolithic and Bronze Ages between 4000 and 1500BC.
- **It was once** thought megaliths began in one place. Now experts think they emerged in many areas.
- **Menhirs** are large standing stones. Sometimes they stand by themselves, sometimes in avenues or circles.
- **The largest** known menhir is the Grand Menhir Brisé at Locmariaquer near Carnac, France. This single stone once stood 20 m tall and weighed 280 tonnes.
- **The largest stone circle** is at Avebury in Wiltshire.
- **The most famous stone circle** is Stonehenge on Salisbury Plain, built between 3100 and 1800BC.

> ★ STAR FACT ★
> The Grand Menhir Brisé is seven times as heavy as the biggest stones at Stonehenge.

▲ *The most famous avenues of stone are at Carnac in Brittany, France, where thousands of stones stand in long lines.*

- **Some megaliths** align with amazing accuracy with astronomical events, such as sunrise at the solstice (midsummer day) and may have acted as calendars.
- **Erecting the stones** took huge teams of men working with wooden rollers, levers and ropes.

Archaeology

- **Archaeology** is the scientific study of relics left by humans in the past, from old bones to ancient temples.
- **Most archeological relics** are buried beneath the ground or sunk beneath the sea.
- **Aerial photography** often shows places to dig. Crops and grass will grow differently if the soil is affected by a buried wall or filled-in ditch.
- **Geophysical surveys** involve using metal detectors and other electronic probes to pick up features underground.
- **Field walking** involves walking over the site, carefully scanning the ground by eye for tiny relics.

▶ *Archeological digging is a very painstaking process. Diggers must work with immense care to avoid missing or breaking tiny, fragile relics.*

- **During a dig,** archaeologists dig carefully down through the layers, noting exactly where every relic was found, in case their position helps to reveal the story.
- **Archaeologists** call on many different kinds of expert to help them interpret finds. Forensic scientists may help tell how a skeleton died, for instance.
- **The deeper** a relic is buried, the older it is likely to be.
- **Radio carbon dating** is a way of dating the remains of once-living things from their carbon content. This is accurate up to 50,000 years ago.
- **Potassium argon dating** helps to date the rocks in which relics were found from their potassium and argon content. Human remains in Africa were dated this way.

The first farms

▲ *Farming began about 11,000 years ago as people began saving grass seed to grow, so they could grind new seed into flour.*

- **Starch marks** on stone implements found in Papua New Guinea suggest yams may have been grown there at least 30,000 years ago.

- **Water chestnuts** and beans may have been farmed near Spirit Cave in north Vietnam from 11,000 to 7,500BC.

- **About 9000BC,** some people abandoned the old way of life, hunting animals and gathering fruit, and settled down to farm in what is called the Neolithic Revolution.

- **Farming began** as people planted grasses for their seed (or grain) in the Near East, in Guangdong in China and in Latin America – and perhaps planted root vegetables in Peru and Indonesia too.

- **Emmer wheat and barley** were grown in the Near East c.8,000BC. Sheep and goats were tamed here soon after.

- **The ox-drawn plough** was used from c.5000BC. The Chinese used hand ploughs even earlier.

- **Crop irrigation canals** were dug at Choya Mami, near Mandali in Iraq, between 5500 and 4750BC.

- **China,** the Indus, Egypt and Babylonia all had extensive irrigation systems by 3000BC.

- **The first farmers** reaped their grain with sickles of flint.

- **Farmers** soon learned to store food. Underground granaries at Ban-Po, Shansi, China, date from c.4800BC.

The first cities

- **The walls** of the city of Jericho on the River Jordan are 11,000 years old, and the city has been continuously occupied longer than anywhere else in the world.

- **People began** to live in towns when farming produced enough extra food for people to specialize in crafts such as basket-making and for people to begin to trade.

- **Villages and towns** probably first developed in the Near East in the Neolithic, about 8000BC.

- **Tells** are mounds built up at ancient settlement sites in the Near and Middle East as mud-brick houses crumble.

- **The most famous** ancient town is Catal Hüyük in Anatolia, in Turkey, which was occupied from 7000 to 5500BC. 10,000 people may have lived here.

- **The houses** in Catal Hüyük were made from mud bricks covered with fine plaster. Some rooms were shrines, with bulls' heads and mother goddesses.

- **Asikli Hüyük** is a nearby forerunner of Catal Hüyük, dating from over a thousand years earlier.

- **The first big city** was Eridu in Mesopotamia (Iraq's Abu Shahrain Tell) which has a temple dating from 4900BC.

- **50,000 people** were living in Sumerian Uruk (modern Warka) on the banks of the Euphrates in Iraq in 3500BC.

- **Sumerian Ur** was the first city to have a population of a quarter of a million, by about 2500BC.

◄ *Houses in Catal Hüyük were so tightly packed people had to walk over flat roofs to get to them, then climb through a hole down ladders.*

Mesopotamia and Sumer

- **Mesopotamia** lies between the Tigris and Euphrates Rivers in Turkey, Syria and Iraq. *Mesopotamia* is Greek for 'between rivers'.

- **Mesopotamia** is called the 'cradle of civilization' because many ancient civilizations arose here, including the Sumerian, Babylonian and Assyrian.

- **The first great civilization** was that of the Sumerians, who farmed irrigated land by the Euphrates c.5000BC and lived in mud-brick houses.

- **By 4000BC,** the settlements of Eridu, Uruk and Ur had grown into towns with water supplies and drainage systems, palaces and temple mounds called ziggurats.

- **Sumerians** devised the first writing system (cuneiform), made with wedge-shaped marks on clay tablets.

◀ No one knows when the wheel was invented. It probably developed from potters' wheels. But by 3200BC carts like this were used in Sumer.

- **Sumerians** cast beautiful objects – first from copper, then, from 3500BC, in bronze.

- The Sumerian *Epic of Gilgamesh* tells of a flood similar to the biblical story of Noah's Ark.

- **The Sumerians** developed the first elaborate systems of government and law.

- **At first each city** or 'city-state' was run by a council of elders, but in wartime a *lugal* (leader) took charge. By 2900BC *lugals* were kings and ruled all the time.

- **In 2350BC** Sumer was overrun by Sargon of Akkad, but Sumerian power was re-established at Ur in 2150BC.

Indus civilization

> ★ STAR FACT ★
> Soapstone trading seals from the Indus have been found as far away as Bahrain and Ur.

- **About 3000BC** a civilization developed from small farming communities in the Indus valley in Pakistan.

- **The remains** of over 100 towns of the Indus civilization have been found. The main sites are Mohenjo-Daro, Harappa, Kalibangan and Lothal.

- **Indus cities** were carefully planned, with straight streets, bath-houses and big granaries.

- **At the centre** was a fortified citadel, built on a platform of bricks. The rulers probably lived here.

- **Indus houses** were built of brick around a central courtyard. They had several rooms, a toilet and a well.

- **The Indus civilization** had its own system of writing, which appears on objects such as carved seals – but no one has yet been able to decipher it.

▶ Seals like this were used by Indus merchants to stamp bales of goods.

- **Single-room** huts at all intersections are thought to be police-posts.

- **Mohenjo-Daro** and Harappa had 35,000 inhabitants each by about 2500BC.

- **By 1750BC** the Indus civilization had declined, perhaps because floods changed the course of the Indus River. War may also have played a part. It finally vanished with the arrival of the Aryans in India about 1500BC.

Great migrations

- **The first migrations** occurred when human-like *Homo ergaster* walked out of Africa 750,000 years ago (ya).

- **Experts once** thought oceans blocked migrations but it now seems boats have been used since the earliest days.

- **100,000 ya** humans moved out of Africa into the Near East.

- **About 50,000 ya** humans began the great expansion that took them to every continent but Antarctica within 20,000 years – and wiped out the Neanderthals.

- **50-40,000 ya,** humans spread across Asia and Australasia. 40-35,000 ya, they moved into Europe. 30-25,000 ya, they trekked out of northeast Asia and crossed into the Americas.

- **Early humans** were mainly nomadic hunters, always on the move, following animals into empty lands.

- **Changes in climate** triggered many migrations. People moved north in warm times and retreated in Ice Ages. When the last Ice Age ended, 10,000 ya, hunters moved north through Europe as the weather warmed. Those left behind in the Middle East settled down to farm.

- **From 9,000-7,000 ya,** farming spread northwest through Europe – partly through people actually moving, partly by word of mouth.

- **4,000 ya,** Indo-European peoples spread out from their home in southern Russia. They went south into Iran (as Mittanians) and India (Aryans), southwest into Turkey (Hittites) and Greece (Mycenaeans) and west (Celts).

- **About 3,000 ya,** the Sahara began to dry up, and people living there moved to the fringes. Bantu people from Nigeria and the Congo spread south through Africa.

▶ *Just like American pioneers in the 1800s, Aryans 4,000 years ago moved their families and possessions in covered wagons, probably pulled by oxen.*

The beginnings of Egypt

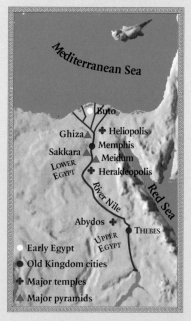

▲ *The Ancient Egyptians built great cities and monuments along the Nile Valley during the Old Kingdom.*

- **While dozens** of cities were developing in Mesopotamia, in Egypt the foundations were being laid for the first great nation.

- **From 5000-3300BC** farmers by the River Nile banded together to dig canals to control the Nile's annual flooding and water their crops.

- **By 3300BC,** Nile farming villages had grown into towns. Rich and powerful kings were buried in big, box-like mud-brick tombs called *mastabas*.

- **Egyptian townspeople** began to work copper and stone, paint vases, weave baskets and use potters' wheels.

- **Early Egypt** was divided into two kingdoms: Upper Egypt, and Lower Egypt on the Nile delta. In 3100BC, King Menes of Upper Egypt conquered Lower Egypt to unite the two kingdoms, but a king of Egypt was always called King of Upper and Lower Egypt.

- **Menes** founded a capital for united Egypt at Memphis.

- **With Menes**, Egypt's Dynasty I – the first family of kings – began. The time of Dynasties I and II, which lasted until 2649BC, is known as the Archaic Period.

- **After the Archaic Period** came the Old Kingdom (2649-2134BC), perhaps the greatest era of Egyptian culture.

- **Craftsmen** made fine things, scholars developed writing and the calendar and studied astronomy and maths.

- **The greatest scholar** and priest was Imhotep, minister to King Zoser (2630-2611BC). Imhotep was architect of the first of the great pyramids, the Step Pyramid at Sakkara.

Babylon

- **Babylon** was one of the greatest cities of the ancient world. It stood on the banks of the Euphrates River, near what is now Al Hillah in Iraq.

- **Babylon** reached its peak in two phases: the Old Babylonian Empire (1792–1234BC) and the New Babylonian Empire (626–539BC).

- **Babylon first** grew as a city from 2200BC, but only when Hammurabi became king in 1792 did it become powerful. In his 42-year reign, Hammurabi's conquests gave Babylon a huge empire in Mesopotamia.

- **Hammurabi** was a great law-maker, and some of his laws were enscribed on a stone pillar, or stele, now in the Louvre in Paris. One of his main laws was that 'the strong shall not oppress the weak'. There were also strong laws to punish crimes and protect people from poor workmanship by builders and doctors.

- **After Hammurabi died,** Babylonian power declined and the Assyrians gained the upper hand. After long Babylonian resistance, the Assyrians destroyed the city in 689BC, only to rebuild it 11 years later.

◄ Under Nebuchadnezzar II (630–562BC), Babylon achieved its greatest fame. He is known for conquering Jerusalem and for his great building projects.

- **Just 60 years or so later,** Babylonian king Nabopolassar and his son Nebuchadnezzar II crushed the Assyrians and built the new Babylonian Empire.

- **Under Nebuchadnezzar II,** Babylon became a vast, magnificent city of 250,000 people, with grand palaces, temples and houses.

- **Babylon** was surrounded by walls 26 m thick – glazed with blue bricks, decorated with dragons, lions and bulls and pierced by eight huge bronze gates. The grandest gate was the Ishtar Gate, which opened on to a paved avenue called the Processional Street.

- **Babylonians** were so sure of their power that King Belshazzar was having a party when the Persians, led by Cyrus, attacked. Cyrus's men dug canals to divert the Euphrates river, then slipped into the city along the river bed. Cyrus wrote on the walls for Belshazzar, 'You are weighed in the balance, and are found wanting.'

> ★ **STAR FACT** ★
> Dying of a fever, Alexander the Great found cool relief in the Hanging Gardens.

▶ The Greeks described the Hanging Gardens of Babylon as one of the Seven Wonders of the ancient world. Nebuchadnezzar II was said to have had them built for his wife Amyitis, who missed the greenery of her mountain home.

Gardens of lush trees and flowers filled rising brick terraces

The gardens were on a huge pyramid of brick and tar, 25 m high

Water for the plants was continually raised from the river by screw pumps wound by slaves

First Chinese emperors

- **In China,** farming communities known as the Yanshao culture developed by the Huang He (Yellow River) 7,000 years ago. By 5000BC, the region was ruled by emperors.

- **Early Chinese emperors** are known of only by legend. Huang-Ti, the Yellow Emperor, was said to have become emperor in 2697BC.

- **In about 2690BC,** Huang-Ti's wife, Hsi-Ling Shi, discovered how to use the cocoon of the silkworm (the caterpillar of the *Bombyx mori* moth) to make silk. Hsi-Ling was afterwards known as Seine-Than (the Silk Goddess).

- **By 2000BC,** the Chinese were making beautiful jade carvings.

▶ *The Shang emperors were warriors. Their soldiers fought in padded bamboo armour.*

- **The Hsias family** were said to be one of the earliest dynasties of Chinese emperors, ruling from 2000 to 1750BC.

- **The Shangs** were the first definitely known dynasty of emperors. They came to power in 1750BC.

- **Shang emperors** had their fortune told every few days from cracks on heated animal bones. Marks on these 'oracle' bones are the oldest examples of Chinese writing.

- **Under the Shangs,** the Chinese became skilled bronze casters.

- **In the Shang cities** of Anyang and Zengzhou, thick-walled palace temples were surrounded at a distance by villages of artisans.

- **Shang emperors** went to their tombs along with their servants and captives as well as entire chariots with their horses and drivers.

Egyptian writing

- **Ancient Egyptian** writing developed between 3300 and 3100BC – perhaps inspired by Sumerian scripts.

- **Egyptian writing** is called hieroglyphic (Greek for 'holy writing'). The Egyptians called it the 'words of the gods', because they believed writing was given by the god Thoth.

- **The last known** hieroglyphs were written in AD394, long after anyone knew how to read them.

- **In AD1799,** the French soldiers of Napoleon's army found a stone slab at Rosetta in Egypt. It was covered in three identical texts in Greek and in two kinds of hieroglyph.

- **In AD1822,** Jean François Champollion deciphered the Rosetta stone, realizing that hieroglyphs are pictures that stand for sounds and letters, not just for objects.

- **There are 700** hieroglyphs. Most are pictures and can be written from left to right, right to left or downwards.

- **Words inside** an oval shape called a *cartouche* are the names of pharaohs.

- **There were two short-hand** versions of hieroglyphs for everyday use – early hieratic script and later demotic script.

- **Egyptians** not only wrote on tomb walls but wrote everyday things with ink and brushes on papyrus (paper made from papyrus reeds) or ostraca (pottery fragments).

- **Only highly trained** scribes could write. Scribes were very well paid and often exempt from taxes.

◀ *The walls of Egyptian tombs are covered in hieroglyphs.*

Egyptian lifestyles

▲ *Egyptian girls were highly conscious of their looks, wearing make-up and jewellery and doing their hair carefully.*

- **Egyptian women** painted their nails with henna and reddened their lips and cheeks with red ochre paste.

- **Egyptian fashions** changed little over thousands of years, and their clothes were usually white linen.

- **Men wrapped linen** round themselves in a kilt. Women wore long, light dresses. Children ran naked in summer.

- **Every Egyptian** wore jewellery. The rich wore gold inlaid with gems; the poor wore copper or faience (made by heating powdered quartz).

- **Egyptians** loved board games. The favourites were *senet* and 'hounds and jackals'.

- **Rich Egyptians** had lavish parties with food and drink, singers, musicians, acrobats and dancing girls.

- **Rich Egyptians** often went fishing or boating.

- **Egyptians** washed every day in the river or with a jug and basin. The rich were given showers by servants.

- **Instead of soap** they used a cleansing cream made from oil, lime and perfume. They also rubbed themselves all over with moisturizing oil.

Ancient Crete

- **The Minoan civilization** of Crete was the first civilization in Europe.

- **Minoan civilization** began about 3000BC, reached its height from 2200 to 1450BC, then mysteriously vanished – perhaps after the volcano on nearby Santorini erupted.

- **The name Minoan** comes from the Greek legend of King Minos. Minos was the son of Europa, the princess seduced by the god Zeus in the shape of a bull.

- **Greek stories** tell how Minos built a labyrinth (maze) in which he kept the Minotaur, a monster with a man's body and a bull's head.

- **Catching a bull** by the horns and leaping over it (bull-leaping) was an important Minoan religious rite.

- **Experts now think Minos** was a title, so every Cretan king was called Minos.

- **The Minoans** were great seafarers and traded all over the eastern Mediterranean.

- **At the centre** of each Minoan town was a palace, such as those found at Knossos, Zakro, Phaestos and Mallia.

- **The largest Minoan palace** is at Knossos, which covered 20,000 square metres and housed over 30,000 people.

- **The walls** of the palace are decorated with frescoes (paintings), which reveal a great deal about the Minoans.

▶ *Knossos had a very good water supply system via long clay pipes. This is the queen's bathroom.*

The pharaohs

Family shrine

Grand reception area where the official did his business for the pharaoh

Well

The central hall was where the official entertained friends

Bedrooms

Kitchen

Wine cellar

Servants' quarters

Stables

Grain stores

▶ The patronage of the pharaohs gave great power and prestige to their officials, who built houses like these around 1200BC.

★ **STAR FACT** ★
People thought the pharaoh could control the weather and make the land fertile.

- **Pharaohs** were the kings of Ancient Egypt. They were also High Priest, head judge and commander of the army.

- **Egyptians** thought of the pharaoh as both the god Horus and the son of the sun god Re. When he died he was transformed into the god Osiris, father of Horus. Since he was a god, anyone approaching him had to crawl.

- **The pharaoh was** thought to be so holy that he could not be addressed directly. Instead, people referred to him indirectly by talking of the pharaoh, which is Egyptian for 'great house'. Only after about 945BC was he addressed directly as the pharaoh.

- **In official documents** the pharaoh had five titles: Horus; Two Ladies; Golden Horus; King of Upper and Lower Egypt and Lord of the Double Land (Upper and Lower Egypt); and Son of Re and Lord of the Diadems.

- **The pharaoh's godlike** status gave him magical powers. His *uraeus* (the snake on his crown) was supposed to spit flames at his enemies and he could trample thousands.

- **There were 31 dynasties** (families) of pharaohs, beginning with Menes in c.3100BC and ending with the Persian kings in 323BC. Each dynasty is identified in order by a Roman numeral. So the fifth Dynasty is Dynasty V.

- **A pharaoh** usually married his eldest sister to keep the royal blood pure. She became queen and was known as the Royal Heiress, but the pharaoh had many other wives. If the pharaoh died while his eldest son was still a child, his queen became regent and ruled on his behalf.

- **To preserve their bodies for ever,** pharaohs were buried inside massive tombs. The first pharaohs were buried in huge pyramids. Because these were often robbed, later pharaohs were buried in tombs cut deep into cliffs.

- **One of the greatest pharaohs** was Ramses II, who ruled from 1290 to 1224BC. He left a legacy of many huge buildings including the rock temple of Abu Simbel.

The Olmecs and Chavins

- **People** began farming in Meso America (Mexico and Central America) 9,000 years ago, almost as long ago as in the Middle East.
- **By 2000BC** there were permanent villages and large farms growing corn, beans, squash and other crops.
- **Between 1200 and 400BC,** a remarkable culture was developed by the Olmecs in western Mexico.

- **The Olmecs** had a counting system and calendar, but no writing system, so little is known about them.
- **Ruins of a huge** Olmec pyramid have been found at La Venta in Tabasco, Mexico.
- **The Olmecs** carved huge 'baby-face' heads from basalt with enormous skill – apparently with only stone chisels, since they had no metal.
- **By 2000BC,** huge religious sites were being built all over what is now Peru.
- **From 800 to 400BC,** the Chavin civilization spread from the religious centre of Chavin de Huantar in the Peruvian mountains.
- **From AD100 to 700,** America's first true city developed at Teotihuacan, with vast pyramids and palaces.
- **Teotihuacan** may have been the world's biggest city in AD300, with a population of over 250,000.

◀ The Olmec heads were carved from huge blocks of volcanic rock weighing up to 14 tonnes. No one knows how they were moved.

Aryan India

- **The Aryans** were a fair-skinned herding people from southern Russia, ancestors to both Greeks and Indians.
- **About 2000BC,** the Aryan people began to sweep through Persia and on into India, where they destroyed the Indus civilizations.
- **The Aryans** were tough warriors who loved music, dancing and chariot racing, but slowly adopted Dravidian gods and settled in villages as farmers.
- **Aryans** were originally split into three classes: Brahmins (priests) at the top, Kshatriya (warriors) in the middle and Vaisyas (merchants and farmers) at the bottom.
- **When they settled** in India, the Aryans added a fourth class, the conquered, dark-skinned Dravidians, who became their servants.
- **From the four Aryan classes,** the elaborate system of castes (classes) in today's India developed.
- **The Aryans** gave India Sanskrit, the ancestor of all India's languages today.

- **Sanskrit** is closely related to European languages such as English, German and Latin.
- **The Aryans** had no form of writing, but they passed on history and religion by word of mouth in spoken Books of Knowledge, or *Vedas*.
- **The Brahmins** created as *Vedas* the first Hindu scriptures, including the *Rig-Veda*, the *Sama-Veda* and *Yajur-Veda*.

▶ The dark-skinned Dravidian people who lived in India when the Aryans arrived became the servant class.

Semites

- **Jewish people** and Arabs are Semitic people.

- **In 2500BC,** the Semites were farming peoples such as the Akkadians, Canaanites and Amorites, who lived in what is now Israel, Jordan and Syria.

- **In 2371BC,** an Akkadian called Sargon seized the throne of the Sumerian city of Kish. He soon conquered all Sumer and Akkad and created a great empire.

- **The Akkadian Empire** collapsed c.2230BC, under attacks from tribes of Gutians from the mountains.

- **From 3000 to 1500BC,** Canaanite Byblos was one of the world's great trading ports, famous for its purple cloth.

- **c.2000BC,** Amorites conquered Sumer, Akkad and Canaan. In 1792BC, the Amorite Hammurabi was ruler of Babylon.

◄ *The Dead Sea Scrolls, on display here, are ancient Hebrew manuscripts found by shepherds in 1947 in a cave near the Dead Sea. They include the oldest known texts of the Bible's Old Testament.*

- **The first Hebrews** were a Semitic tribe from southern Mesopotamia. Their name meant 'people of the other side' of the Euphrates River.

- **According** to the Bible, the first Hebrew was Abraham, a shepherd who lived in the Sumerian city of Ur, 4,000 years ago. He led his family first to Syria, then to Canaan (now Palestine), where he settled.

- **Abraham's grandson** Jacob was also called Israel and the Hebrews were afterwards called Israelites.

- **About 1000BC,** the Israelites prospered under three kings – Saul, David and Solomon.

The Assyrians

- **The Assyrians** came originally from the upper Tigris valley around the cities of Ashur, Nineveh and Arbela.

- **c.2000BC,** Assyria was invaded by Amorites. Under a line of Amorite kings, Assyria built up a huge empire. King Adadnirari I called himself 'King of Everything'.

- **The Old Assyrian Empire** lasted six centuries, until it was broken up by horsemen from a place called Mittani.

> **★ STAR FACT ★**
> King Assurbanipal's (668-627BC) palace was filled with books and plants from all over the world.

- **From 1114 to 1076BC,** King Tiglath Pileser I rebuilt Assyrian power by conquest, creating the New Assyrian Empire.

- **The New Assyrian Empire** reached its peak under Tiglath-Pileser III (744-727BC) and was finally overthrown by the Medes and Babylonians in 612BC.

- **The Assyrians** were ruthless warriors. They grew beards and fought with bows, iron swords, spears and chariots.

- **The Assyrians** built good roads all over their empire, so that the army could move fast to quell trouble.

- **The Assyrians** built magnificent palaces and cities such as Khorsabad and Nimrud.

- **Arab warriors** rode camels into battle for the Assyrians.

◄ *Statues of winged bulls with human heads were found at Nimrud.*

Oceania

- **The people** of the Pacific may have been the greatest seafarers of the ancient world.

- **Up until 5,000 years ago,** the sea was lower and Tasmania, Australia and New Guinea were all part of one big continent.

- **About 50,000 years ago,** bold, seafaring people crossed the ocean from Southeast Asia and settled in Australia.

- **Most early sites** are now lost offshore under the sea, which rose to cut off New Guinea and Australia c.5000BC.

- **The Australian** aboriginals are descendants of these original inhabitants.

- **The oldest settlement** in New Guinea is 40,000 years old.

- **c.4000BC,** domesticated plants and animals reached New Guinea from Asia, and farmers drained fields at Kuk Swamp. But many people remained hunters.

- **About 2000BC,** people sailed in canoes from Indonesia to colonize Melanesia and Micronesia – the islands of the western Pacific, such as Vanuatu.

▲ *The people of Oceania crossed the oceans in canoes like these tens of thousands of years before the great European explorers.*

- **Early Melanesians** are known by their 'Lapita' pottery, which originated in the Molucca Islands of Indonesia.

- **Rowing canoes** seen in a 50,000-year-old cave painting in Australia match those seen all over the Pacific – and in caves in the Amazon jungle.

Dead Egyptians

- **Egyptians saw death** as a step on the way to a fuller life in the Next World.

- **Everyone was thought** to have three souls: the *ka*, *ba* and *akh*. For these to be well, the body must survive intact, so the Egyptians tried to preserve the body.

- **Gradually,** the Egyptians developed embalming techniques to preserve the bodies of kings and rich people who could afford it.

- **The organs** were cut out and stored in 'canopic jars' and the body dried with natron (salt).

- **The dried body** was filled with sawdust, resin and natron, then wrapped in bandages. The embalmed body is a 'mummy'.

- **A portrait** mask was put over the mummy's head, then it was put in a coffin.

- **Anthropoid (human-shaped)** coffins were used from about 2000BC onwards. Often, the mummy was put inside a nest of two or three coffins, each carved and painted and perhaps decorated with gold and gems.

- **The wooden coffin** was laid inside a stone coffin or sarcophagus inside the burial chamber.

- **At first,** the prayers said for a dead ruler were carved on pyramid walls as 'Pyramid Texts'. Later, they were put on coffins as 'Coffin Texts'. From 1500BC, they were written on papyrus in the *Book of the Dead*.

- **To help him** overcome various tests and make it to the Next World, a dead man needed amulets and a *Book of the Dead*, containing magic spells and a map.

◄ *When placing the mask over the mummy, the chief embalmer wore a mask representing the jackal god Anubis.*

Persia

- **Iran** is named after the Aryan people who began settling there in c.15,000BC. Two Aryan tribes – the Medes and Persians – soon became dominant.

- **In 670BC,** the Medes under King Cyaxeres joined forces with the Babylonians to finally overthrow the Assyrians.

- **In 550BC,** the Medes themselves were overthrown by the Persians. The Persian king Cyrus II was the grandson of the king of the Medes, Astyages.

- **Cyrus II** had an army of horsemen and very skilled archers. He went on to establish a great Persian empire after conquering Lydia and Babylon.

- **The Persian Empire** was ruled by the Achaemenid family until it was destroyed by Alexander the Great in 330BC.

◄ Darius the Great ruled Persia from 521 until 486BC.

- **The Persian Empire** reached its greatest extent under Darius I, who called himself Shahanshah ('King of kings'). Darius introduced gold and silver coins, and also brought chickens to the Middle East.

- **Darius built** a famous road system and split his empire into 20 *satrapies* (regions), each ruled by a *satrap*.

- **'King's Ears'** were officials who travelled around and reported trouble back to the king.

- **The Persians** built luxurious cities and palaces, first at Susa, then in Darius's reign, at Persepolis.

- **Persian priests,** or magi, were known for their magic skills, and gave us the word 'magic'. A famous magus called Zarathustra, unusually, worshipped a single god: Ahuru Mazda. His god's evil enemy was Angra Mainyu.

Weapons of war

- **Early stone axes and spears** may have been used both for hunting and as weapons. Remains of a half-a-million year-old wooden spear were found at Boxgrove, England.

- **A spear-thrower** was a stick with a notch in one end to take the end of a spear. With it, hunters (or fighters) could hurl a spear with tremendous force. Spear-throwers were the first ever machines made by humans, c.35,000BC.

▼ The chariot was the airforce of the ancient civilizations, speeding archers and spear-throwers across the battlefield. Egyptians, Hittites and Assyrians fought huge battles with thousands of chariots.

- **The first pictures** of bows come from North Africa, c.15,000-30,000BC. Bows could be devastatingly effective and were the main weapons of the earliest civilizations.

- **The invention** of bronze, c.3000BC, meant people could make metal swords, daggers, axes and spears.

- **A tiny bronze statue** of a chariot found at Tell Agrab, Iraq, dates from 3000BC. This is the first image of a chariot.

- **The Persian emperor** Cyrus (559-529BC) added scythes (long, sharp blades) poking out from chariot wheels to slice through the legs of enemy soldiers and horses.

- **The oldest helmet** (c.2500BC), made of a gold and silver alloy called electrum, was found in the royal tombs of Ur.

- **The crossbow** was invented in the Greek colony of Syracuse, about 400BC.

- **Alexander the Great** used giant crossbows firing 5 m arrows to win his empire between 340 and 323BC.

- **Around AD100,** Dionysius of Alexander in Egypt invented a rapid-firing crossbow, able to fire dozens of bolts a minute.

Tutankhamun

- **Tutankhamun** was pharaoh (king) of Ancient Egypt from 1347 to 1339BC. He was a boy when he became pharaoh and only 18 when he died.

- **Tutankhamun** was the last of the great 18th dynasty (family) of pharaohs who ruled Egypt 1567-1339BC. They included the warrior queen Hatshepsut, and Thutmose III, who led Egypt to the peak of its power around 1400BC.

- **Tutankhamun** was the son of Akhenaten, who with his queen Nefertiti created a revolution in Egypt. Akhenaten replaced worship of the old Egyptian gods with worship of a single god, and moved the capital to Armarna.

- **Tutankhamun's wife** was his half-sister Ankhesenamun. When he died – perhaps murdered – Ankhesenamun was at the mercy of his enemies, Ay and general Horemheb. She wrote to the Hittite king asking for his son to marry, but the Hittite prince was murdered on the way to Egypt. Ankhesenamun was forced to marry Ay, who thus became pharaoh. She also died young.

- **The Valley of the Kings** near Luxor on the Nile in Egypt is the world's greatest archaeological site. It was the special burial place of the 18th dynasty pharaohs and contains the tombs of 62 pharaohs, and high officials.

- **Tutankhamun's** tomb was the only tomb in the Valley of the Kings not plundered over the centuries. When opened, it contained 5,000 items, including many fabulous carved and gold items.

- **Tutankhamun's** tomb was discovered by the English archaeologist Howard Carter, in 1922.

- **Rumours of a curse** on those disturbing the tomb began when Carter's pet canary was eaten by a cobra – the pharaoh's symbol – at the moment the tomb was opened.

- **Experts** worked out the dates of Tutankhamun's reign from the date labels on wine-jars left in the tomb.

◀ A fabulous gold mask was found in the innermost coffin, over the badly mummified remains of the young king. The skull showed signs of a fracture from a hammer.

In the burial chamber were four shrines of gilded wood, one inside the other

Inside the shrines, there was a red sandstone sarcophagus (coffin)

Inside the sarcophagus, there were three gold coffins, one inside the other

Beyond the burial chamber was a treasury full of gold and other treasures

Fabulous beds, chests, gold chariot wheels, and carved animals in the anteroom were just a taste of the riches to come

▶ When Carter opened Tutankhamun's tomb, he came first to an anteroom. It took him three years to clear this room and enter the burial chamber, with its huge gold shrines containing the coffins.

The Trojan Wars

- **From 1600 to 1100BC,** mainland Greece was dominated by tough warrior people called the Mycenaeans.

- **The Mycenaeans** fought with long bronze swords, long leather shields and bronze armour.

- **Mycenaeans** lived in small kingdoms, each with its own fortified hilltop city or *acropolis*.

- **A typical Mycenaean noble** was like a Viking chieftain. In the middle of his palace was a great hall with a central fireplace where warriors would sit around telling tales of heroic deeds.

- **After 1500BC** Mycenaean kings were buried in a beehive-shaped tomb called a *tholos*, with a long, corridor-shaped entrance.

▶ *Troy fell when the Greeks pretended to give up and go home, leaving behind a huge wooden horse. The jubilant Trojans dragged this into the city – only to discover Greeks hiding inside it.*

- **The Greek poet Homer** tells how a city called Troy was destroyed by the Mycenaeans after a ten-year siege. Historians once thought this was just a story, but now the remains of Troy have been discovered, they think there may be some truth in it.

- **The Trojan War** in Homer's tale is caused by the beautiful Helen of Sparta. She married Menalaus, brother of King Agamemnon of Mycenae, but she fell in love with Prince Paris of Troy.

- **Helen and Paris** eloped to Troy and Agamemnon and other Greeks laid siege to Troy to take her back.

- **The battle** featured many heroes – such as Hector, Achilles and Odysseus.

- **The Greeks** finally captured Troy when Greek soldiers hidden inside a wooden horse found their way into the city.

Early Greece

- **Around 1200BC,** the Mycenaeans began to abandon their cities, and a people called the Dorians took over Greece.

- **Many Mycenaeans** fled overseas in a large battle fleet, and the Egyptians called them the Sea Peoples. Some ended up in Italy and may have been the ancestors of the Etruscan people there.

- **With the end** of Mycenaean civilization, Greece entered the Dark Ages as the art of writing was lost.

- **About 800BC,** the Greeks began to emerge from the Dark Ages as they re-learned writing from the Phoenicians, a people who traded in the eastern Mediterranean.

- **The period** of Greek history from 800 to 500BC is called the Archaic (Ancient) Period.

- **In the Archaic Period,** the Greek population grew rapidly. States were governed by a few rich aristocrats.

- **The early Greeks** loved athletics and held four major events. They were called the Panhellenic Games and drew competitors from all over the Greek world.

- **The four Panhellenic Games** were the Olympic, Pythian, Isthmian and Nemean Games.

- **The Olympic Games** started in 776BC and were the most important. They were held every four years at Olympia.

- **The Greek poet Homer** wrote his famous poems about the Trojan Wars between 850 and 750BC.

◀ *A Greek house may have looked something like this 2,600 years ago, with first-floor bedrooms surrounding a courtyard.*

The Mayans

◄ *The Mayan pyramid at Chichén Itzá in the Yucatán.*

- **The Mayans** were a people who dominated Central America for 2,500 years until 1441.

- **The Mayans** began building large pyramids with small temples on top between 600BC and AD250.

- **Mayan civilization** peaked between AD250 and 900. This is called the Classic Period.

- **During the Classic Period,** Mayan civilization centred on great cities such as Tikal in the Guatemalan lowlands. They traded far and wide on foot and in dug-out canoes.

★ STAR FACT ★
The Mayans were brilliant astronomers and believed that the stars linked them to their gods.

- **Mayans in the Classic Period** developed a clever form of writing in symbols representing sounds or ideas. They recorded their history on stone monuments called *stelae*.

- **Mysteriously,** around AD800, the Mayans stopped making *stelae* and the Guatemalan cities were abandoned.

- **From AD800 to 1200,** the most powerful Mayan city was Chichén Itzá in the Yucatán region. From 1200 to 1440 another city, Mayapan, came to the fore. After 1440, Mayan civilization rapidly broke up, though no-one knows why.

- **The Mayans** were deeply religious. Deer, dogs, turkeys and even humans were often sacrificed to the gods in the temples on top of the pyramids.

- **Mayan farmers** grew mainly corn, beans and squash. From the corn, women made flat pancakes now called tortillas, and an alcoholic drink called *balche*.

Confucius

- **Confucius** is the most famous thinker and teacher in Chinese history.

- **Confucius** is the name used by Europeans. Chinese people called him Kongzi or K'ung-Fu-Tzu.

- **Confucius was born** in Lu, now Shantung Province, in 551BC, traditionally on 28 September, and died in 479BC.

- **Confucius mastered** the six Chinese arts – ritual, music, archery, charioteering, calligraphy (writing) and arithmetic – and became a brilliant teacher.

- **Confucius** was the first person in China to argue that all men should be educated to make the world a better place, and that teaching could be a way of life.

- **In middle age,** Confucius served as a minister for the King of Lu. He had a highly moral approach to public service. He told statesmen this golden rule: 'Do not do to others what you would not have them do to you.'

- **The King of Lu** was not interested in Confucius's ideas, so Confucius went into exile, followed by his students.

- **After his death,** Confucius's sayings were repeated. His ideas were developed by teachers like Mencius (390-305BC) and Xunzi (c.250BC) into a way of life called Confucianism.Until recently, this dominated Chinese life.

- **Living at the same** time as Confucius may have been a man called Laozi. Laozi wrote the *Tao Te Ching*, the basis of Taoist religion.

- **The *Tao Te Ching*** tells of the *Tao* (Way) – the underlying unity of nature that makes everything what it is.

▶ *Confucius's belief was that court officials should not plot for power but study music, poetry and the history of their ancestors.*

Chinese technology

- **Western experts** have only recently realized that ancient Chinese technology was very advanced, and many of their early inventions only reached Europe thousands of years later.

- **In the early 1600s,** the great English thinker Francis Bacon said that three quite recent inventions had changed the world – printing, gunpowder and the ship's magnetic compass. All of these had been invented in China a thousand or more years earlier.

- **The world's oldest surviving** printed book is the *Diamond Sutra*, printed in China about AD868. But printing in China goes back to at least the 7th century AD.

- **The world's first robot** was an amazing ancient Chinese cart with gears from the wheels that turned a statue on top so that its finger always pointed south.

- **The Chinese** had alcoholic spirits 2,000 years ago, over a thousand years before they came to Europe.

- **The horse stirrup** was invented in China in the 3rd century BC. This gave horse-soldiers a steady platform to fight from and allowed them to wear heavy armour.

- **The wheelbarrow** was invented by the Chinese c.100BC.

- **Cast-iron ploughs** were made in China around 200BC.

- **Football** was invented in China. About 200BC, they were playing a game called *t'su chu*. It involved kicking an inflated leather ball through a hole in a silk net.

▶ The Chinese made a magnetic compass called a sinan over 2,000 years ago. A ladle made of a magnetic stone called lodestone spins round on a shiny bronze plate to point south.

▶ The Chinese discovered gunpowder and made the first guns about 1,100 years ago. They also became famous for their fireworks.

▲ One particularly nasty Chinese invention was the 'Heaven-Rumbling Thunderclap Fierce Fire Erupter'. This was a gunpowder-fired device that shot out shells of poisonous gas.

▲ Acupuncture involves sticking pins in certain points on the body to treat illness. The Chinese used it 1,800 years ago – but it may have been used earlier in Europe .

◀ In AD132, Chang Heng made the world's first earthquake detector with a special jar. When even a faint, distant quake occurred, a metal ball would fall with a clang from the dragon's mouth at the top of the jar into the toad's mouth.

◀ The Chinese invented mechanical clocks in AD723 – 600 years earlier than Europe. This is Su Sung's 'Cosmic Engine', an amazing 10-m-high clock built at Khaifeng in AD1090.

▶ Water-powered machines for spinning cloth are often thought of as inventions of the English Industrial Revolution in the 1700s. In fact, the Chinese were building them at least 500 years earlier, to spin a cloth called ramie.

The search for Troy

- **Troy is the city** in the Ancient Greek poet Homer's famous epic, the *Iliad*. It was once thought to be entirely mythical.

- **In 1822,** British scholar Charles McClaren suggested that Homer's Troy might be in Turkey. He pinpointed a mound called Hisarlik near the Dardanelles – a narrow sea linking the Black Sea and the Aegean.

- **German archaeologist** Heinrich Schliemann began digging at Hisarlik mound in 1871.

- **In 1873,** Schliemann uncovered fortifications and remains of a very ancient city, which he believed to be Troy.

- **Schliemann** also found a treasure of gold and silver which he called Priam's treasure after the Trojan King Priam mentioned in the *Iliad*. He smuggled this out of Turkey to take to Europe.

◄ *When Schliemann found this gold mask at Mycenae, in 1876, he thought it must be Agamemnon's. In fact, it dates from 300 years earlier.*

- **In 1876,** Schliemann was digging at Mycenae in Greece. He found what he thought was the tomb of Agamemnon, king of the Trojans' enemies in the *Iliad*.

- **In the 1890s,** Wilhelm Dorpfield showed that Hisarlik mound is made of nine layers of city remains. This is because the city was destroyed by fire or earthquake nine times. Each time the survivors built on the rubble.

- **Schliemann** thought Homer's Troy was Troy II (2), second layer from the bottom. Dorpfield thought it was Troy VI.

- **Troy I to V** (1 to 5) are now thought to date from the early Bronze Age (c.3000 to 1900BC).

- **Experts** now think Homer's Troy may be Troy VII, a layer of the seventh city, dating from about 1250BC.

Greek city-states

- **Ancient Greece** was not a single country in its early days, but a collection of independent cities or city-states.

- **A Greek city-state** was called a *polis* (plural *poleis*).

- **Polis** gives us the words politics and police – and polite.

- **There were several hundred** *poleis* in Ancient Greece. The largest were Athens and Sparta.

- **Each city** typically had a mound called an *acropolis* with a temple on top, and a market place called an *agora*.

★ **STAR FACT** ★
The laws of the Athenian oligarch Draco were so harsh that severe laws are still called draconian.

- **To start with** (from about 800 to 600BC), city-states were governed by oligarchs (a few powerful men) or a tyrant, but people gradually got more say.

- **People in Greek city-states** were either free or slaves. Free men (not women) were split into citizens (born in the city itself) and *metics* (immigrants).

- **In 508BC,** a man called Cleisthenes gave Athens a new system of government called democracy.

- **Democracy** comes from the Greek word *demos* (people) and *kratos* (rule). The idea was that every citizen (but not metics and slaves) had the right to speak and vote in the Assembly, held every ten days on a hill called the Pnyx.

◄ *The most famous acropolis is the Acropolis in Athens with the Parthenon temple on top, but nearly every polis had one.*

Zhou and Qin dynasties

- **c.1100BC**, the Shang in China were conquered by a people called the Zhou.

- **The Zhou** extended the Shang's territory far across China, but the kingdom was divided into large estates, each with its own ruler.

- **In the time of the Zhou,** the Chinese began using iron, both for ploughs and weapons, and made many advances in technology.

- **Great thinkers** such as Laozi and Confucius came to the fore.

- **Confucius** believed morals were vital in government service, but a minister called Shang Yang (who died 338BC) thought the law must be strengthened by any means. This is called Legalism.

- **Shang Yang's** family – the Qin – overthrew the Zhou in 312BC.

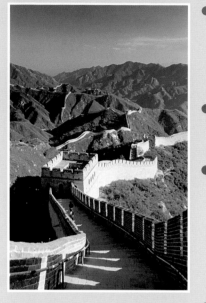

▲ *Although today's brick and stone wall dates from the 1400s, the Great Wall of China was first built of earth bricks in 214BC, under Shi Huangdi.*

- **In 246BC,** Qin emperor Zheng expanded the empire and called himself Shi Huangdi, First Emperor. He had the 4,000-km-long Great Wall built to protect his empire from nomads from the north.

- **Shi Huangdi** banned books and buried 460 Confucian scholars alive. His eldest son Fu Su was banished when he objected.

- **When Shi Huangdi** died, in 210BC, his body was taken secretly to the capital by minister Li Si with a fish cart to hide the smell of rotting flesh. Li Si sent a letter to Fu Su, pretending it was from his father, telling him to commit suicide. Fu Su did and so Li Si came to power.

- **Shi Huangdi** was buried with an army of 6,000 life-size clay soldiers, called the Terracotta Army when found in 1974. Parts of the tomb are said to be booby-trapped.

Famous generals

▶ *Hannibal's greatest feat was leading an army – with elephants – through Spain and then the Alps in winter to attack Rome from the north.*

- **In 2300BC** King Sargon of Akkadia led his soldiers to victory over much larger armies by using especially far-shooting bows.

- **Tuthmose III** (1490-1436BC) was perhaps the greatest of the warrior pharaohs, fighting 17 campaigns and taking Egypt to its greatest extent.

- **Assurbanipal** (669-627BC) was the great Assyrian leader whose chariots gave him a powerful empire from the Nile to the Caucasus Mountains.

- **Sun-Tzu** was the Chinese military genius who, in 500BC, wrote the first manual on the art of war.

- **Alexander the Great** was the Macedonian whose army of 35,000 was the most efficient yet seen – and who perfected the phalanx.

- **Hannibal** (247-182BC) was the greatest general of the powerful city of Carthage (now near Tunis in Africa).

- **Scipio** (237-183BC) was the Roman general who conquered Spain and broke Carthaginian power in Africa.

- **Julius Caesar** was the greatest Roman general.

- **Belisarius** (AD505-565) and Narses (AD478-573) were generals for Byzantine Emperor Justinian. Their mounted archers defeated the Vandals and Goths.

- **Charles Martel** (AD688-741), 'the Hammer', was the Frankish king who defeated the Moors at Tours in France in AD732 and turned back the Arab conquest of Europe.

Buddha

- **Buddha** was the founder of the Buddhist religion, who lived in India c.563-483BC.
- **Buddha's** real name was Siddhartha Gautama.
- **Buddha** is not a name but a title (like the messiah) meaning 'enlightened one', so you should really say 'the Buddha'.
- **Archaeological excavations** finished in 1995 suggest that a man who may have been Siddhartha lived in the palace of his father Suddodhana on what is now the border of Nepal and India.
- **As a young prince,** Siddhartha lived a life of luxury. When he was 16 years old, he married his cousin the Princess Yasodhara, who was also 16 years old.

◀ *Most statues of the Buddha show him sitting cross-legged deeply meditating (thinking).*

- **The turning point** was when Siddhartha was 29 and he saw four visions: an old man, a sick man, a corpse and a wandering holy man.
- **The first three visions** told Siddhartha that life involved ageing, sickness and death. The fourth told him he must leave his wife and become a holy man.
- **After six years of** self-denial, Siddhartha sat down under a shady 'bo' tree to think – and after several hours the answer came to him.
- **The Buddha** spent the rest of his life preaching his message around India.
- **The Buddha** died at the age of 80. His bones became sacred relics.

Greek thinkers

◀ *Aristotle, the brilliant tutor to Alexander the Great, was thought of as the ultimate authority on every subject for over 2,000 years.*

- **The great thinkers** of Ancient Greece were called philosophers. Philosophy is Greek for 'love of wisdom'.
- **The key philosophers** were Socrates, Plato and Aristotle.
- **Socrates** (466-399BC) believed people would behave well if they knew what good behaviour was and challenged people to think about truth, good and evil.
- **Plato** (427-348BC) argued that, behind the messy chaos of everyday experience, there is a perfect and beautiful Idea or Form. He also tried to find the ideal way of governing a state.
- **Aristotle** (384-322BC) argued that, for true knowledge, you must find the 'final cause' – why something happens.

- **Aristotle** was the first great scientist, stressing the need to collect data, sort the results and interpret them.
- **Many of the basic** ideas in philosophy, even today, come from Socrates, Plato and Aristotle, and other Greek philosophers such as Epicurus and Diogenes.
- **Greek mathematicians** such as Euclid, Appolonius, Pythagoras and Archimedes worked out many of our basic rules of maths. Most school geometry still depends on the system devised by Euclid.
- **Greek astronomers** like Aristarchus and Anaxagoras made many brilliant deductions – but many of these were forgotten. Aristarchus realized that the Earth turned on its axis and circled the Sun. Yet it was almost 2,000 years before this idea was generally accepted.

> ★ STAR FACT ★
> Archimedes showed how the effect of a lever could be worked out by maths.

Homer

- **Homer** is the Ancient Greek poet said to have written the ancient world's two greatest poems: the *Iliad* and the *Odyssey*.

- **Homer probably** lived in the 9th century BC in Ionia, on what is now the Aegean coast of Turkey, or on the island of Chios.

- **No one knows** for certain if Homer existed, or if he composed all of both poems. Most experts think he did.

- **In Homer's time** there was a great tradition of bards. These were poets who recited aloud great tales of heroic deeds. They knew the poems by heart and so never wrote them down.

- **The *Iliad* and the *Odyssey*** are the only poems from the times of the bards that were written down and so survive. They may have been written down at the time, or later.

- **After Homer's time** the two great poems were used in religious festivals in Greece.

◀ *Nothing is known about Homer, but legend says he was blind.*

- **For centuries** after Homer's time, Greek children learned to read, and learned about the legends of the past, by studying Homer's two great poems.

- **In the 2nd century BC,** scholars at the Alexandrian Library in Egypt studied the poems. A few scholars came to the conclusion that they were so different in style they must have been written by two different poets.

- **The *Iliad*** is a long poem in lofty language about the Trojan Wars, in which the Greeks besiege the city of Troy to take back the kidnapped Helen.

- **The *Odyssey*** tells the amazing adventures of hero Odysseus on a great journey.

Early Americans

▲ *Carving wooden duck decoys for hunting is a North American tradition dating back thousands of years.*

- **The Americas** were the last continents humans occupied.

- **The first Americans** may have been Australian aboriginals who arrived by boat 50,000 years ago.

- **Ancestors of today's Native Americans** probably came to the Americas 20-35,000 years ago, from Asia. They are thought to have walked across the strip of land that once joined Asia and North America across the Bering Strait.

> **! NEWS FLASH !**
> A 50,000 year-old skull found in Colombia resembles the skulls of Australian aboriginals.

- **By 6000BC, the first Native Americans** had spread south from Alaska and far down into South America.

- **There is evidence** that humans were living in Mexico over 20,000 years ago. At El Jobo in Colombia, pendants dating back to 14,920BC have been found.

- **10,000 years ago,** groups of 'Paleo-Indians' on North America's Great Plains hunted now-extinct animals such as camels and mammoths. In the dry western mountains, Desert peoples planted wild grass-seed.

- **In Mexico,** people began to grow squash, peppers and beans at least 8,500 years ago.

- **Corn was probably first** grown around 5,600 years ago.

- **Corn, beans and squash** provided food for early American civilizations such as the Olmecs and Mayans.

Greek art

A chorus linked the scenes with verse and songs

The circular acting area was called the orchestra

A typical theatre, like the Theatre of Dionysus in Athens, seated 14,000 in stadium-like rows

Scenes were played by just two or three actors, each wearing a mask

Audiences took cushions to sit on and picnics to keep them going

Behind the orchestra was a house or 'skene' where the actors changed. Later this became a backdrop.

▶ Formal drama was developed in Ancient Greece in the 5th and 6th centuries BC. Huge audiences watched plays in open-air arenas.

In later Greek theatres, the skene developed side wings here called paraskinia

- **In the heyday of Ancient Greece,** thousands of sculptors, architects, painters, dramatists and poets were creating a fantastic wealth of beautiful works of art.

- **The Greeks** made graceful statues and friezes to decorate temples and homes. They were carved mostly from marble and limestone and then painted, though in surviving statues the paint has worn away.

- **The most famous sculptors** were Phidias (c.490-420BC), Praxiteles (c.330BC), Lysippus (c.380-306BC) and Myron (c.500-440BC). Phidias's huge gold and ivory statue of the god Zeus was famous throughout the ancient world.

- **Greek architects** such as Ictinus and Callicrates created beautiful marble and limestone temples fronted by graceful columns and elegant triangular friezes. The most famous is the Parthenon in Athens.

- **The Greeks** had three styles for columns: the simple Doric, the slender Ionic, topped by scrolls, and the ornate Corinthian, topped by sculpted acanthus leaves.

- **The style** created by the Greek temples is now called Classical and has influenced architects ever since.

- **The Greeks** believed each art was inspired by one of nine goddesses called Muses.

- **Ancient Greek writers** include the poets Homer, Sappho and Pindar. They created styles of writing including epic poetry.

- **The tragedy** is a grand drama doomed to end unhappily for the hero. Tragedy was created by Greek dramatists such as Aeschylus, Euripides and Sophocles, who wrote the tragedy King Oedipus.

★ STAR FACT ★
The Colossus of Rhodes was a huge 37-m-high statue cast in bronze by Greek sculptor Chares. It stood astride the entrance to the harbour of Rhodes in the Aegean.

▶ The famous Venus de Milo was found on the Aegean island of Milos in AD 1820. It was carved in Greek Antioch (now in Turkey) around 150BC and shows the goddess of love Aphrodite (Roman goddess Venus). The statue originally had arms.

What people ate

- **1.5 million years ago,** people learned how to use fire to cook food. The oldest known cooking fire is at Swartkrans, South Africa.

- **The first ovens** were pits for hot coals, first used in the Ukraine about 20,000 years ago. The first real ovens were from Sumer and Egypt, c.2600BC.

- **Grain seeds** were cooked and mixed with water to make gruel (porridge). c.20,000 years ago, people learned to bake gruel on a hot stone to make flat bread, like pitta.

- **Pottery** meant liquids could be heated to make stews. The oldest pottery is 13,000-year-old pots from Odai-Yamomoto in Japan. The first pots from the Near East, from Iran, date back 11,000 years.

- **c.12,000 years ago,** people found how to make food last by letting it ferment, making cheese from milk and wine from grapes.

- ▶ *The earliest people simply ate what food they could find – either by hunting (like fish) or gathering (like berries).*

- ◀ *Bread was the first processed food, made by baking ground-up grass seeds mixed with water.*

- **c.8000BC,** people began to farm animals such as sheep and grow plants such as cereals for food. Diets became less varied than when people gathered food wild, but much more reliable.

- **c.4000BC** special farmers in Palestine were growing oil-rich olives to squeeze and make olive oil in huge amounts. Romans consumed vast quantities.

- **c.2600BC,** the Egyptians found that, by leaving gruel to ferment, they could make a dough. This they baked in ovens to make the first raised bread.

- **Honey** was the main sweetener. Egyptians kept bees for honey and also made sweet syrups from fruits.

- **The oldest recipe book** is an Assyrian stone tablet from 1700BC with 25 recipes, including a bird called a *tarru* cooked in onion, garlic, milk and spices.

The Phoenicians

- **From about 3000BC,** Semitic peoples such as Canaanites lived on the eastern Mediterranean coast and built the great city of Byblos.

- **From about 1100BC,** the people living here became known as Phoenicians.

- **The word 'phoenicians'** comes from *phoinix*, the Greek word for a purple dye made famous by these people.

- ▶ *Phoenicians were master seafarers. Broad merchant ships called gaulos carried goods. Fifty-oared rowing galleys like this defended the ports from attack.*

Hull built from the famed cedars of Lebanon trees

- **The Phoenicians** were great sea traders. Their ports, of Tyre and Sidon bustled with ships carrying goods from all over the known world.

- **The Phoenicians** used wool from Mesopotamia and flax and linen from Egypt to make cloth. They also made jewellery from imported gems, metals and ivory.

- **Phoenicians** invented the alphabet and gave us the word too. The Phoenician words *aleph* ('ox') and *beth* ('house') became the Greek letters *alpha* and *beta*. The word Bible and the prefix *bibli-* (meaning 'books') come from Byblos.

- **The dye** for which the Phoenicians were famous was made from the shells of murex snails.

- **c.600BC,** Phoenician sailors sailed from the Red Sea right round Africa and back into the Mediterranean.

- **Phoenicians** set up colonies across the Mediterranean as far west as Gades (now Cadiz, in Spain).

- **The greatest** Phoenician colony was the city of Carthage in what is now Tunisia.

Polynesians

- **Polynesians** are the people who live on the islands in the middle of the Pacific Ocean, from Hawaii to Easter Island and New Zealand.

- **There are 10,000** islands in Polynesia and the rest of the eastern Pacific, with hundreds of different cultures and languages, each with its own history.

- **Many Polynesian islands** may well have been first settled 40,000 years ago by people from Southeast Asia.

- **2,000 years ago,** a second wave of migrants moved east from Fiji, Samoa and Tonga to the Marquesas Islands.

- **The settlers** crossed the ocean in small double canoes and outriggers.

- **In their canoes** the settlers took crops (coconuts, yams, taros and breadfruit) and livestock (pigs and chickens).

> ★ STAR FACT ★
> The biggest *moai* statues on Easter Island are
> up to 12 m tall and weigh 90 tonnes.

▲ There are about 600 huge stone *moai* statues on Easter Island, on platforms called ahus. No one knows what they were for.

- **Every island** developed its own style of woodcarving.

- **About AD400,** the new Polynesians moved on to Hawaii and Easter Island.

- **Easter Islanders** created strange stone statues called *moais*, carved with stone tools since they had no metal.

Greek gods and myths

- **The Greeks** had a wealth of myths – stories about their gods, goddesses, heroes and villains.

- **We know** about the myths mainly from Homer's poems and Hesiod's book *Theogeny*, both from about 700BC.

- **Theogeny** tells how the Earth began, with the earth goddess Gaia emerging from chaos and giving birth to Uranus, the king of the sky.

- **The many children** of Gaia and Uranus were called the Titans, led by Cronos.

- **Cronos** married his sister Rhea. Their children, led by Zeus, rebelled against the Titans to become the new top gods, called the Olympians.

- **The Olympians** were said to live on Mt Olympus, and include the most famous Greek gods, such as Apollo the god of light, Demeter the goddess of crops, Artemis the goddess of the Moon and Dionysius the wine god.

- **Greek heroes** were mostly heroes from the times of the Trojan Wars or earlier.

- **Early heroes** include Jason, who led his Argonauts (his crew) in search of the fabulous Golden Fleece, and Theseus, who killed the minotaur.

- **Trojan war heroes** included Achilles and Odysseus.

- **The greatest hero** was super-strong Heracles, whom the Romans later called Hercules.

◀ The Romans adopted many Greek gods. These are Venus (Greek goddess Aphrodite), the goddess of love, and Mercury (Hermes) the winged foot-messenger.

Alexander the Great

▶ In just nine years and a series of brilliant campaigns, Alexander created a vast empire. No one knows exactly what his plans were. However, the teachings of his tutor Aristotle were important to him, and he had his own vision of different peoples living together in friendship.

MACEDONIA

Gordium

Mediterranean

Alexandria

SYRIA

EGYPT

Babylon

PERSIA

Persepolis

Samarkand

Hindu Kush

Indus River

INDIA

Indian Ocean

← Alexander's route

● **Alexander the Great** was a young Macedonian king who was one of the greatest generals in history. He built an empire stretching from Greece to India.

> ★ STAR FACT ★
> An old legend said that anyone who untied a tricky knot in a town called Gordium would conquer Asia. Alexander instantly sliced through this Gordian knot with his sword.

● **Alexander** was born in 356BC in Pella, capital of Macedonia. His father King Phillip II was a tough fighter who conquered neighbouring Greece. His mother was the fiery Olympias, who told him that he was descended from Achilles, the hero of the *Iliad*.

● **As a boy,** he was tutored by the famous philosopher Aristotle. A story tells how he tamed the great unridable horse Bucephalus, which afterwards carried him as far as India.

● **When Alexander was 20,** his father was murdered by a bodyguard and he became king. Alexander quickly stamped out rebellion.

▶ The key to Macedonian success was the phalanx. In a phalanx, armoured soldiers stood in tightly packed rows bristling with long spears. Such a formation could withstand a cavalry attack, yet still move swiftly.

● **In 334BC,** Alexander crossed the narrow neck of sea separating Europe from Asia with his army. Within a year, he had conquered the mighty Persian Empire.

● **In 331BC,** Alexander led his army on into Egypt where he was made pharaoh and founded the city of Alexandria. He trekked on to the desert oasis of Siwah where legend says an oracle proclaimed him son of the god Zeus.

● **In 327BC,** he married the lovely Bactrian princess, Roxane.

● **After capturing** the city of Babylon and finishing off Persian King Darius, Alexander led his conquering army into India. Here his homesick troops finally asked to go home.

● **In 325BC, Alexander had** ships built and carried his army down the Indus River and returned to Babylon. Within a year, he fell ill and died.

The founding of Rome

- **People lived** in Italy long before Rome was founded and a people called the Etruscans created an advanced civilization in the northwest between 800 and 400BC.

- **According to legend,** Rome was founded in 753BC by the twins Romulus and Remus, who were said to have been brought up by a she-wolf.

- **By 550BC,** Rome was a big city ruled by Etruscan kings.

- **In 509BC,** the Roman people drove out the kings and made themselves an independent republic.

- **Republican Rome** was ruled by the Senate, an assembly made up of 100 patricians (men from leading families).

- **In theory,** Rome was governed by the people. But real power was in the hands of patricians; plebeians (ordinary citizens) had little. Slaves had no power or rights at all.

- **Plebeians** fought for power and, by 287BC, gained the right to stand as consuls, the highest official posts.

- **In the 400s** and 300s BC, Rome extended its power all over Italy by brute force and alliances.

▲ Legend has it that Rome was founded by the twins Romulus and Remus, who were brought up by a she-wolf.

- **By 264BC,** Rome rivalled Carthage, the North African city that dominated the western Mediterranean. In 164BC, Rome destroyed Carthage totally after the Punic Wars.

- **By 130BC** Rome had built a mighty empire stretching from Spain to Turkey and along the North African coast.

Cleopatra

- **Cleopatra** (69-30BC) was the last Macedonian queen of Egypt. She was descended from Ptolemy, a general of Alexander the Great who made himself king after Alexander died.

- **Cleopatra may** have been beautiful. She was certainly intelligent, charming and highly determined.

- **Cleopatra** became queen in 51BC, when her father died. Her ten-year-old brother Ptolemy became king.

- **Ptolemy's guardians** seized power and drove Cleopatra out. She was restored to the throne by the Roman armies of Julius Caesar.

- **Legend has it** that Cleopatra had herself delivered to Caesar rolled up in a carpet. Whatever the truth, he fell in love with her, and she had a son, Caesarion, by him.

- **Caesar** invited Cleopatra and Caesarion to Rome, where she stayed until 44BC, when Caesar was assassinated.

◀ Octavian described Cleopatra as a wicked temptress and the idea has stuck. But her people in Egypt thought of her as a great, just and much-loved queen.

- **The Roman general** Mark Antony went to Cleopatra for her support in his bid for power in Rome. He too fell in love with her. They later married and had three children.

- **Mark Antony** returned to Rome to make a political marriage to Octavia, sister of Octavian. But he soon returned to Cleopatra.

- **Mark Antony and Cleopatra** were ambitious and strove to take over the eastern Roman Empire. But their armies were defeated at the Battle of Actium, off Greece, in 31BC by the forces of Octavian (later Augustus Caesar).

- **As Octavian** chased them to Alexandria, Cleopatra spread rumours that she was dead. In despair, Mark Antony stabbed himself. He died in her arms. Cleopatra tried to make peace with Octavian but failed. She took her life by placing an asp, a poisonous snake, on her breast.

The rise of Rome

- **As Rome's** empire spread, the creation of plantations worked by slaves put small farmers out of work. The gap between rich and poor widened.

- **Many joined** the army to escape poverty and became more loyal to their generals than to the Senate.

- **Two popular generals,** Pompey and Julius Caesar, used their armies to take over Rome and suspend the Republic.

- **Caesar and Pompey** argued, and after battles right across the empire, Caesar gained the upper hand.

◀ Many Romans lived in comfortable two-storey townhouses (domi), with heated pools and underfloor heating.

- **Once in power,** Caesar restored order and passed laws to reduce people's debts.

- **Caesar** was made dictator and ruled Rome without the Senate.

- **In 44BC,** a man called Brutus killed Caesar to restore the Republic – but Caesar's place was taken by another general, Octavian, Caesar's adopted son.

- **By 27BC,** Octavian was so powerful he declared himself the first Roman Emperor and took the name Augustus.

- **Under Augustus,** rebellious parts of Spain and the Alps were brought under control and the empire was expanded along the Rhine and Danube Rivers.

- **By 1BC,** the days of strife were over and Rome presided over a vast, stable, prosperous empire.

Jesus

- **Jesus Christ** was one of the world's great religious leaders. The religion of Christianity is based on his teachings.

- **Our knowledge** of Jesus's life comes almost entirely from four short books in the Bible's New Testament: the gospels of Matthew, Mark, Luke and John.

- **Roman writers** such as Pliny mention Jesus briefly.

- **Jesus** was born in Bethlehem in Palestine between 4 and 1BC.

◀ Jesus is his own name. Christ is a title that comes from the Greek word christos, which means 'anointed one'.

- **The Bible** tells how his poor young virgin mother Mary became miraculously pregnant after a visit by the archangel Gabriel, and that Jesus is the only Son of God.

- **Little** is known of Jesus's childhood. His teaching began after he was baptized by John the Baptist at the age of 30.

- **Jesus's mission** was to announce that the Kingdom of God was coming. From his many followers, he chose 12 'apostles' to help him spread the word.

- **Jesus performed** all kinds of miracles to convince people of the truth of his teachings.

- **Many Jews** felt Jesus was a troublemaker, especially after a triumphal entry into Jerusalem. They had the Roman governor Pontius Pilate put him to death by crucifixion (nailing to a cross).

★ STAR FACT ★
After his death, Jesus was said to have been resurrected – brought to life again.

The Han dynasty

- **In 210BC,** the small Han kingdom was ruled over by Liu Bang. Liu Bang was a poor villager who had come to power as the Qin Empire broke down.

- **In 206BC,** Liu Bang led an army on the Qin capital, Xiangyang. He looted Shi Huangdi's tomb, and burned the city and the library containing the books Shi Huangdi had banned – the only existing copies.

- **In 202BC,** Liu Bang proclaimed himself first Han emperor and took the name Gaozu.

- **Under the Han,** China became as large and powerful as the Roman Empire, and art and science thrived. Chinese people still sometimes call themselves Han.

- **Under Wudi** (141–87BC), Han China reached its peak.

- **Han cities** were huge, crowded and beautiful, and craftsmen made many exquisite things from wood, paint and silk – sadly destroyed when Han rule ended.

- **Silk, jade and horses** were traded along the Silk Route, through Asia as far as the Roman Empire.

▶ *Beautiful objects like this bronze urn were traded between China and Europe along the famous Silk Route for thousands of years.*

- **Han emperors** tried to recover the lost writings and revived the teachings of Confucius. Public officials became scholars and in 165BC the first exams for entry into public service were held.

- **About AD50,** Buddhist missionaries reached China.

- **By AD200,** the Han emperors were weakened by their ambitious wives and eunuchs (guardians). Rebellions by a group called the Yellow Turbans, combined with attacks by warriors from the north, brought the empire down.

Roman towns

- **Roman towns** were the biggest and most sophisticated the world had seen. They were not built on rigid grids like Greek cities, but they all had common features.

- **Roman towns** had two main streets and many side streets with spaces in between called *insulae* (islands).

- **The *insulae*** were tightly packed with private houses – houses of the rich called *domi* and apartment blocks (also called *insulae*). The bigger houses had courtyards.

- **Traffic jams** were so common that many towns banned wheeled traffic from the streets during daylight.

- **Most towns** had numerous shops, inns (*tabernae*), cafés (*thermopilia*) and bakeries (*pistrina*).

- **The forum** was a large open market and meeting place surrounded on three sides by a covered walkway. The fourth side was the law courts and town hall (*basilica*).

- **Most towns** had many grand temples to Roman gods.

- **Most towns** had a large open-air theatre. There was also a games arena or stadium where warriors called gladiators fought and chariot races were held.

- **The bath houses** (*thermae*) were places where people came to sit around and dip into hot and cold baths in magnificent surroundings.

- **Towns** had very good water supplies and sewage systems.

◀ *The remains of the forum in Rome give a glimpse of just how magnificent Roman cities must have been.*

The Roman Empire

▲ Gladiators were prisoners and criminals who were made to fight in big arenas called amphitheatres to entertain people.

◀ This map shows the empire at its peak under the Emperor Trajan (AD98-117). It was divided into areas called provinces, such as Britannia (England and Wales) and Gallia (northern France). Each had its own Roman governor, often a retired consul (minister), who used his power to extort taxes.

- **For 200 years** after Augustus became emperor in 27BC, Roman emperors ruled over an empire so large and secure that citizens could talk of the *Pax Romana* (Roman Peace).

- **The Romans** built straight roads to move their troops about quickly. On the whole, they governed peacefully and also built hundreds of towns in the Roman manner.

- **After Augustus** died, in AD14, his stepson Tiberius succeeded him. Then came a succession of Augustus's descendants, including Gaius, Claudius and Nero.

- **Gaius** (AD37-41) was known as Caligula ('little boots') because of the soldiers' boots he wore as a child.

- **Soon after** Caligula became emperor, an illness left him mad. He spent wildly, had people whipped and killed, married and murdered his sister and elected his horse as a minister. Eventually he was murdered by soldiers.

- **Claudius** (AD41-54) replaced Caligula. People thought he was stupid because he stuttered and was crippled. But he proved the wisest and most humane of all emperors.

- **Claudius** was probably poisoned by his 4th wife Agrippina, who wanted power for her son Nero.

- **The power of Roman emperors** reached a peak under the 'Antonines' – Nerva, Trajan, Hadrian, Antoninus and Marcus Aurelius. They ruled AD96-180.

- **The empire** grew only a little after Augustus. Britain was conquered in AD43, and Trajan took Dacia (now Hungary and Romania).

> ★ **STAR FACT** ★
> Roman historian Suetonius claimed Nero sang and played the lyre during Rome's great fire in AD64.

▶ Leading imperial officials wore distinctive flowing robes called togas, with a strip dyed in a rare purple called Tyrian purple. Laws were written on papyrus or parchment.

The Roman army

- **Rome owed its power** to its highly efficient army.

- **In a crisis,** Rome could raise an army of 800,000 men.

- **The Roman army** fought mainly on foot, advancing in tight squares bristling with spears and protected by large shields called *scutari*. They often put shields over their heads to protect them from arrows. This formation was called a *testudo* or tortoise.

- **Under the Republic,** the army was divided into legions of 5,000 soldiers. Legions were made of 10 cohorts. Cohorts were made of centuries of 80-100 soldiers.

- **Each legion** was led by a *legatus*. A cohort was led by a *tribunus militum*. A century was led by a centurion.

- **All Roman soldiers** had a short sword (60 cm long) and carried two throwing spears. They also wore armour – first, vests of chain mail and a leather helmet; later, metal strips on a leather tunic and a metal helmet.

- **Roman armies** built huge siege engines and catapults called *ballistas* when they had to capture a town.

- **After 100BC,** most soldiers were professionals, who joined the army for life. Food took about a third of their wages.

- **In training,** soldiers went on forced 30 km marches three times a month. They moved at 8 km per hour, carrying very heavy packs.

- **Soldiers** were flogged for misbehaviour. Mutiny was punished by executing one in ten suspects. This was called decimation.

▶ *The tough Roman soldier marched carrying all his weapons and armour, plus a heavy pack full of clothes, food and tools for digging and building.*

The Roman way of life

- **In big cities,** rich Romans had a comfortable way of life.

- **For breakfast,** Romans typically ate bread or wheat biscuits with honey, dates or olives, and water or wine.

- **A Roman lunch** (*prandium*) consisted of much the same things as breakfast.

- **Romans had** *cena* (the main meal) in the afternoon, after a visit to the baths. This became a very lavish affair with three main courses, each with many dishes.

> ★ **STAR FACT** ★
> The Circus Maximus chariot racetrack in Rome held up to 250,000 spectators.

- **Rich Romans** had a lot of free time, since slaves did all the work. Leisure activities included gambling by tossing coins (*capita et navia*) and knucklebones (*tali*).

- **Public entertainments** were called *ludi* (games). They included theatre, chariot races, and fights with gladiators (trained fighters) and animals.

- **The Emperor Trajan** went to a gladiator contest that lasted 117 days and involved 10,000 gladiators.

- **Romans** had more slaves than any empire in history. Many were treated cruelly, but some lived quite well.

- **In 90BC,** a man called Spartacus led a revolt of slaves that lasted two years, until crushed by Roman armies.

◀ *Romans were very clean and often went to the public baths or bathed at home. These are the Roman baths at Bath, England.*

Famous disasters

▲ *The Greek island of Santorini was blown apart in 1500BC by a giant volcanic eruption, so ending the Minoan civilization.*

- **Many ancient civilizations** had legends of great floods.

- **In the Middle East,** a Sumerian named Ziusudra, the Babylonian Gilgamesh and the Jewish Noah all built an ark (boat) to ride out a flood that drowned all others.

- **In India,** Manu, the first man and first king, was warned by fish and survived the great flood by building a boat.

- **In the Americas,** the Aztecs believed four previous worlds had been destroyed by jaguars, hurricanes, thunder and lightning and a huge 52-year flood.

- **The huge eruption** of the Aegean island volcano of Thera (Santorini), in 1500BC, effectively destroyed Minoan civilization on Crete – and may have started legends of the lost civilization of Atlantis, drowned by a tidal wave.

- **While the Jews** were slaves there, Egypt was ruined by a flood of blood predicted by the Jew Moses – now thought to have been the Nile River in flood, stained by red algae.

- **In 464BC,** 10,000 were killed by an earthquake that rocked the Greek city of Sparta.

- **In 436BC,** a famine drove thousands of Romans to jump into the Tiber River to escape the pain of starvation.

- **In AD64,** the Rome of Emperor Nero was destroyed by a great fire. Angry people said that Nero had started it.

- **In AD79,** the Roman city of Pompeii was buried under ash from nearby volcano Vesuvius – and preserved to this day.

Yamato

- **The oldest signs** of farming in Japan date back to 300BC, but Japan was inhabited long before that.

- **The first known inhabitants** of Japan were the Ainu or Ezo, who were short, hairy, fair-skinned people. Some Ainu people still survive in northern Japan.

- **About 250BC,** the Yayoi tribe became dominant in Japan. They used iron and bronze.

◀ *Shinto priests believe that all things that inspire awe – from twisted trees to dead warriors – have kami (spirits).*

- **In AD167,** priestess Himiko unified Japan under her rule.

- **Himiko** sent ambassadors to China for support, and imported many Chinese ideas.

- **From AD200-645,** the Yamato tribe dominated Japan. The Yamato conquered Korea and were the first emperors.

- **Right up to today,** Japanese emperors claim to be descended from the Yamato, who, in turn, claimed to be descended from the Shinto sun-goddess, Amaterasu.

- **Shotoku Taishi** (AD574-622) was a young regent for old Empress Suiko. He gave Japan organized Chinese-style government and promoted Buddhism and Confucianism.

- **Shinto** or 'way of the gods' has been Japan's religion since prehistoric times. It got its name in the 6th century to distinguish it from Buddhism and Confucianism.

! NEWS FLASH !
In AD2000, the postholes of a round hut half a million years old were found in Japan.

The Mauryan Empire

- **In 321BC,** the first great Indian empire was created by Chandragupta Maurya (c.325-297BC). Its capital was Pataliputra on the Ganges.
- **The Mauryan Empire** at its peak included most of modern Pakistan, Bangladesh and India – except for the very southern tip.
- **The most famous** Mauryan emperor was Chandragupta's grandson Asoka (c.265-238BC).
- **After witnessing** a horrific battle, Asoka was so appalled by the suffering that he resolved never to go to war. He devoted himself to improving the lot of his people.
- **Asoka** became a Buddhist and his government promoted the *Dharma*, or 'Universal Law'.

▲ During Asoka's reign, stupas (domed shrines) containing relics of the Buddha were built all over India.

- **The Universal Law** preached religious tolerance, non-violence and respect for the dignity of every single person.
- **Asoka's men** dug wells and built reservoirs all over India to help the poor. They also provided comfortable rest-houses and planted shady banyan trees for travellers along the new roads.
- **Asoka said** 'all men are my children', and sent officials out to deal with local problems.
- **A vast secret police force** and an army of 700,000 helped Asoka to run his empire.
- **Asoka's** Sarnath lion insignia is now India's national emblem.

Early North Americans

- **Maize** was grown in southwestern USA c.2000-1000BC.
- **The first farming villages** in the southwest were those of the Anasazi, Mogollon and Hohokam peoples and dated from AD100. They lived either in caves or in underground 'pit houses' carved into the desert rock.
- **Anasazi** is Navajo Indian for 'Ancient Ones'.
- **The first Anasazi** are also known as Basket Makers because of their skill in weaving baskets.
- **About AD700,** the Anasazi began to build large stone villages called *pueblos*, which is why from this time they are also called Pueblo Indians.
- **In the 'Classic' Pueblo** period, from AD1050-1300, the Anasazi lived in huge apartments carved out of cliffs, like Pueblo Bonito. Pueblo culture began to fade c.AD1300.

> ★ STAR FACT ★
> Cliff Palace in Mesa Verde had space for 250 people in its 217 rooms.

▲ The most famous cliff pueblos are in Mesa Verde, Colorado.

- **In the east,** the first farming villages were those of the Hopewell peoples of the Illinois and Ohio valleys, between 100BC and AD200.
- **The Hopewell people** are known for their burial mounds. Things found in these mounds show they traded all over America.
- **About AD700,** farming villages with temple mounds developed near St Louis on the Mississippi.

Early Ireland

- **Ireland** was settled late. The first proof of settlers are 8,000-year-old flints left by hunters and fishers on beaches in the northeast, near the modern town Larne.

- **The New Stone Age** (Neolithic) began when the first farms and permanent homes appeared, 5,000 years ago.

- **Neolithic people** honoured their dead with long mounds or barrows – called 'court graves' because they have a courtyard at the entrance. They also built barrows called portal graves with three huge stones set like a door.

- **The most dramatic remains** from earliest times are 'passage' graves. Inside an earth mound a long passage leads to a stone chamber. Of 150 in Ireland, the most famous is Newgrange in the Boyne valley near Dublin.

- **The Celts** invaded Ireland in the Iron Age, about 400BC, and many of Ireland's rich collection of heroic myths are probably based in this time.

▼ The huge burial mound at Newgrange was built around 3100BC. A long, narrow passage leads to a burial chamber deep inside the mound. Above the entrance is an unusual 'roof-box' – a special slot through which the midwinter sun shines into the chamber.

> ★ STAR FACT ★
> The passage tomb on Knocknarea in Sligo is said to be the burial-place of the legendary Queen Maeve.

- **Celtic Ireland** was split into 150 kingdoms or clans called *tuatha* and later into five provinces – Ulster, Meath, Leinster, Munster and Connaught. After AD500, there was a high king (*ard-ri*) ruling Ireland from Tara in Leinster.

- **Irish Celts** were both warriors and herdsmen who valued cows highly. They also revered poets (*file*), and their metalwork, revealed in items such as the Tara brooch and the Ardagh chalice, is extraordinarily beautiful.

- **Early Celtic priests** were druids, but in AD432, St Patrick, legend says, came to convert Ireland to Christianity.

- **Irish monasteries** became havens of art and learning in the Dark Ages, creating the famous *Book of Kells*.

Every year, at exactly 8.58 am on 21 December (the winter solstice), the rising sun shines through this roof-box and right down the passage to light up the burial chamber

One of Newgrange's most distinctive features is the rich ornamentation – especially the carved spirals, which must have had some ritual significance

Julius Caesar

- **Julius Caesar** (c.100-44BC) was Rome's most famous general and leader. He was also a great speaker who had the power to excite huge crowds.

- **Caesar's** individuality was clear from the start. At 17, he defied Sulla, the dictator of Rome and married Cornelia, the daughter of the rebel leader Cinna. Cornelia died when Caesar was about 30.

- **Caesar** began as a politician and made himself popular by spending his own money on public entertainments.

- **In 60BC,** he formed a powerful triumvirate (threesome) with Crassus and Pompey, which dominated Rome.

- **In 58BC,** Caesar led a brilliant campaign to conquer Gaul (now northern France), and invaded Britain.

◀ *Caesar was not only a brilliant general, but a great statesman who brought in many reforms and tried to stamp out corruption.*

- **Caesar** wrote an account of his campaigns in Gaul that is a classic of historical writing.

- **Pompey** was alarmed by the fame that Caesar's conquests brought him. The two began a war that lasted five years, ending in Egypt in 48BC, where Caesar met and fell in love with Cleopatra.

- **By 45BC,** Caesar was undisputed master of the Roman Empire. The people elected him dictator for life.

- **Caesar** was asked to become king, but he refused.

- **On 15 March 44BC** – called the Ides of March – Caesar was stabbed to death as he entered the Senate. His assassins were a group led by Brutus and Cassius, who felt that his ambitions were a threat to Rome.

The Guptas

- **The Guptas** were a family of rulers who reigned in northern India from AD320-c.500. This is India's golden age, with writing, sculpture and other arts at their peak.

- **The Guptas** were originally a family of rich landowners, who took over control of the small kingdom of Magadha in the Ganges valley.

- **Chandragupta I** came to the throne in AD320. He widened his lands by marrying the right women.

- **Chandragupta's** son Samudragupta and his grandson Chandragupta II gained control over much of northern India by military conquests.

- **The Hindu and Buddhist** religions both began to flourish during the Gupta period.

- **Beautiful temples** and religious sculptures were created all over northern India.

- **About AD450,** Kalidása, India's greatest poet and dramatist, wrote his famous play *Sákuntala*, filled with romance and adventure.

- **Music and dance** developed their highest classical form.

- **Hindu mathematicians** developed the decimal system (counting in tens) that we use today.

- **Gupta power** collapsed by about AD500 under repeated attacks by Huns from the north.

▼ *The Hindu and Buddhist sculpture and painting of the Gupta period has been the model for Indian art down the centuries.*

Gauls and Franks

- **The Gauls** were a Celtic people who lived in Western Europe, mainly in France.
- **The Gauls** could be brave warriors, and because the men had long hair and beards, the Romans thought them wild.
- **In 390BC,** Gauls crossed the Alps, swept down on Rome and sacked the city. They later withdrew, but they occupied northern Italy for almost 200 years.
- **In 278BC,** Gauls invaded what is now Turkey, settling the area called Galatia.
- **In the 50s BC,** Julius Caesar led a lightning Roman campaign to crush the Gauls. What is now France became Roman Gaul.

> ★ STAR FACT ★
> Franks were outnumbered 20 to 1 by Gallo-Romans – but France is named after them.

- ◀ In 52BC, the Gallic chief Vercingetorix led a last-ditch attempt to drive out the Romans. But he was beaten, taken to Rome as Caesar's prize and executed.
- **The Franks** were a German people split into two branches, the Salians and Ripurians.
- **In AD486,** Clovis, a king of the Salian Franks, invaded Roman Gaul to create a big kingdom covering modern France and Belgium.
- **The first period** of Frankish rule in Gaul is called Merovingian (from 486 to 751); the second is called Carolingian (751-987).
- **After Clovis's death** in 511, the Merovingian kingdom was divided and weakened. About 719, some Merovingian kings allowed a man called Charles Martel – *martel* means hammer – to take control in the north as 'Mayor of the Palace'. Martel soon controlled the whole of Gaul.

Early African civilizations

- **The first civilizations** appeared in Africa along the Nile valley, in Egypt and further south in Nubia.
- **The first Nubian civilization,** called the A-group culture, appeared about 3200BC in the north of Nubia, known as Wawat. It was taken over by the Egyptians in 2950BC.
- **About 2000BC,** a new Nubian culture emerged in the then-fertile south, called Kush. Unlike the Wawat Nubians, who were Asian, the Kushites were black Africans.

◀ Africa was the birthplace of humanity, and rock paintings dating back 30,000 years are found all over Africa.

- **Egypt** conquered Kush in 1500BC, but the Kushites, led by King Shabaka, conquered Egypt in 715BC. For 50 years, the Kushites were pharaohs and their capital Napata was the centre of the ancient world.
- **In 666BC, Assyrians** drove the Kushites out of Egypt. But from the Assyrians, the Kushites learned iron-making.
- **Napata** had iron-ore, but little wood for smelting the ore. So the Kushites moved their capital to Meroe, where they built great palaces, temples, baths and pyramids.
- **From Kush,** iron-making spread west to Nigeria.
- **From AD100, the city of Axum** – now in northern Ethiopia – grew rich and powerful on ivory. About AD350, the Axumite king Aezanas invaded and overthrew Kush.
- **Kings of Axum** (later Ethiopia) were said to be descended from Jewish King Solomon and the Queen of Sheba. The Sheba were an Arab people who had settled in Axum.
- **King Aezanas** was converted to Christianity, but for 1,500 years Axum/Ethiopia was Africa's only Christian country.

The Celts

▶ *Created in the early 800s in Iona and Ireland, the Book of Kells is one of the great treasures of Celtic art.*

- **The Celts** are an ancient group of peoples who first appeared in the Danube valley in Germany about 3,300 years ago.

- **The first Celts** are known as the Urnfield culture, because they put their cremated dead in urns.

- **From 800 to 400BC,** Celts spread across northern Europe, taking over what is now France as Gauls, England as Britons and Ireland as Gaels.

- **The first wave** of expansion is called Halstatt culture. With bronze, the Celts developed supreme metal-working skills.

- **c.500BC,** Celts learned to make iron and came into contact with Greeks and Etruscans. The 'La Tene' culture emerged.

- **In La Tene,** the distinctive Celtic swirls and spiral decoration appeared on weapons and ornaments.

- **After Gauls** sacked Rome, in 390, it seemed Celts might over-run Europe. But they were split into many tribes, and from 200BC they were pushed ever further west.

- **Some early Celts** used Greek letters to write in their own language, but our knowledge of them comes mostly from Greek and Roman authors.

- **The Celts** were fierce warriors who charged into battle shouting, naked and stained with blue woad dye. But they valued poets higher than warriors. Their poets' tales of heroes and magic tell us how rich their culture was.

- **Celtic clan society** was highly organized and revolved around a clan's chief, who made the laws.

The first Britons

- **Britain** has been inhabited by human-like creatures for over 500,000 years. The oldest known settlement, at Star Carr in Yorkshire, dates back 10,000 years.

- **About 6-7,000 years ago,** Neolithic farmers arrived from Europe. They began to clear the island's thick woods to grow crops and build houses in stone.

- **The early farmers** created round monuments of stones and wooden posts called henges. The most famous is Stonehenge in Wiltshire.

- **c.2300BC,** new people from the Rhine arrived. They are called Beakerfolk, after their beaker-shaped pottery cups. They were Britain's first metal-workers.

- **Legend has it** that the name Britain came from Brutus, one of the sons of Aeneas, who fled from Troy.

- **c.700BC,** Celts arrived, often living in hillforts.

- **Iron axes** and ploughs enabled huge areas to be cleared and farmed, and the population rose.

- **When Julius Caesar** invaded, in 55 or 54BC, the Celtic people of England, called Britons, were divided into scores of tribes, such as the Catuvellauni and Atrebates.

- **Resistance** from tribal leaders such as Caratacus meant it took the Romans over a century to conquer the Britons.

- **The last resistance** was that of Queen Boudicca, in AD60.

▼ *People of Bronze Age Britain lived in round houses like this, with thick stone walls and a steeply-pitched, thatched roof.*

A central hearth kept the house remarkably warm

The fall of Rome

- **After the death** of Marcus Aurelius, in AD180, Rome was beset by political struggles.

- **The Praetorian Guard** (the emperor's personal soldiers) chose or deposed emperors at will, and there were 60 emperors between AD235 and 284 alone.

- **The Empire fell** into anarchy and was beset by famine, plague and invasion.

- **Diocletian** (emperor from 284) tried to make the empire easier to govern by splitting it in two halves – East and West. He asked Maximian to rule the west.

- **Diocletian** retired 'to grow cabbages' at his palace in Dalmatia, and soldiers tried to choose a new emperor.

- **Constantine,** commander of the Roman armies in Britain, defeated his rivals to become emperor. It is said that before the main battle, he saw a Christian cross in the sky. After his victory, he became Christian.

- **In AD330,** Constantine made Byzantium (now Istanbul) his capital and called it Constantinople.

▶ After the emperor Constantine moved his capital there in AD330, Byzantium (now Istanbul in Turkey) became the main defender of Roman civilization.

- **After Constantine's death,** the empire fell into chaos again. It became split permanently into East and West.

- **The Western empire** suffered attacks from barbarians. Vandals invaded Spain and North Africa. Goths and Huns such as Attila attacked from the North.

- **In AD410,** Visigoths led by Alaric invaded Italy and sacked (burned and looted) Rome. In AD455, Vandals sacked Rome again. In AD476, the Western empire finally collapsed.

The spread of Christianity

- **The first Christians** were Jews in Palestine, but followers like Paul soon spread the faith to gentiles (non-Jews) and countries beyond Palestine.

- **At first,** Roman rulers tolerated Christians, but after AD64, they saw Christians as a threat and persecuted them.

- **Persecution** strengthened Christianity by creating martyrs such as St Alban.

◀ Early Christian texts were manuscripts (hand-written) and monks spent years illuminating (decorating) them. The illuminated manuscripts of this time are among the most beautiful books ever made.

- **In 313,** Emperor Constantine gave Christians freedom of worship and called the first great ecumenical (general) church council in 325.

- **By 392,** Christianity was the official religion of the empire.

- **When the Roman Empire** split into East and West, so too did Christianity, with the West focused on Rome and the East on Constantinople.

- **The head of the Western church** was the pope; the head of the Eastern church was called the patriarch. The first pope was Jesus's apostle St Peter, and there has been an unbroken line of popes ever since. But the power of the popes really began with St Gregory, in 590.

- **To separate themselves** from the official religion, some Christians, such as St Benedict, began to live apart as monks in monasteries.

- **After AD500,** monks spread Christianity over NW Europe.

- **Monasteries** became the main havens for learning in the West in the Dark Ages, which followed the fall of Rome.

The Byzantine Empire

The Hippodrome was based on the Circus Maximus in Rome

60,000 spectators watched chariot races here

Four great bronze horses by the emperor's seat at the Hippodrome were stolen by Crusaders and are now on St Mark's Cathedral, Venice

Incredibly thick walls protected the city

The Hagia Sophia, now a museum, is the world's oldest Christian cathedral

A massive aqueduct (water channel) kept the city well supplied with water

▲ At its height, Constantinople was graced by some of the ancient world's most magnificent buildings – including the Hippodrome and the Hagia Sophia. This is the tranquil palace quarter. The rest of the city was noisy and crowded.

> ★ STAR FACT ★
> 29 of Byzantium's 88 emperors died violent deaths, and the endless conspiracies at court have given us the word Byzantine for dark intrigues.

- **When Rome collapsed,** in 476, Constantinople (now Istanbul in Turkey) became the capital of what is now called the Byzantine Empire. It became the centre of Western civilization for the next thousand years.

- **In the six years** after Constantine made Byzantium his capital Constantinople, builders, architects and artists created one of the world's most magnificent cities.

- **Constantinople** was at the focus of trade routes between Asia and Europe. Silks, gems and ivories were traded for gold, grain, olives and wine. By charging ten per cent on all goods coming in and out, the city became fabulously rich.

- **When the great emperor Justinian I** came to the throne in 527, he tried to rebuild the Roman Empire. His general, Belisarius, reconquered Italy, and by 565 the Byzantine Empire stretched right round the Mediterranean.

- **Justinian** also built hundreds of churches, including the famous Hagia Sophia.

- **Justinian** modernized Roman law to create the basis of all western legal systems. This is called the Code of Justinian.

- **The Byzantine Empire** was under constant attack – from Goths, Huns, Persians, Avars, Bulgars, Slavs, Vikings, Arabs, Berbers, Turks, Crusaders and Normans. But it repelled attackers, often with its secret weapon 'Greek fire', invented in 650. This was a mix of quick-lime, petrol and sulphur, which burst into flames when it hit water.

- **In 1204,** Constantinople was ransacked by Crusader knights who were short of money. Almost every treasure in the city was stolen and it never recovered from this devastating blow. The city's population dwindled from 1 million to just 60,000 over the next 200 years.

- **Constantinople** was finally conquered by the Turkish Sultan Mehmet II in 1453.

▶ Justinian I was the greatest Byzantine emperor, although his general's secretary, Procopius, described him as 'a demon incarnate'. He ruled with his beautiful former actress wife, Theodora. Justinian relied on her for support and advice, and it was she who changed laws to improve the lives of women and the poor.

The Sui; Tang and Song

▶ *Gunpowder was invented in the Tang era. The Chinese used it first to make fabulous fireworks and later weapons.*

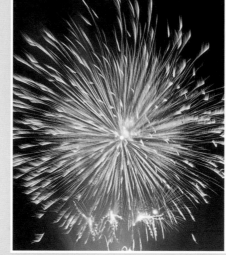

- **In 581** Yang Chien seized the throne in the north of China, founding the Sui dynasty.

- **Yang Chien** conquered the south and reunited China for the first time since the fall of the Han in 220.

- **Under the second** Sui emperor Yang Di, China's Grand Canal was rebuilt on an huge scale, linking China's main rivers. Other canals completed the network.

- **Yang Di** was betrayed by one of his 3,000 mistresses and strangled in 618. Li Yuan, an ambitious Sui minister, then seized the throne to found the Tang dynasty.

- **Under the Tang** trade grew, China became rich again and the arts and sciences flourished.

- **By 751** China was the world's largest empire and the capital Chang'an was the world's largest city, with over a million inhabitants.

- **Chinese people** began to drink tea and sit on chairs.

- **Poets such** as Li Po (701-762) wrote of his love of wild mountains and the fleeting nature of happiness. China's tradition of great landscape painting began and the first printed book, *The Diamond Sutra*, was made in 868.

- **By 800,** the Tang dynasty was beginning to break up, Chang'an declined and China descended into turmoil.

- **Order was restored** in 960 when the Song family began to rule from the city of Kaifeng. The Song lasted until 1276, when the Mongol Kublai Khan conquered China.

Barbarians

▶ *Alaric was the great Gothic leader who took Rome in 410. He lies buried with the treasures he took from Rome in the bed of the Busentius River.*

- **Barbarians** is what the Romans called all the peoples living outside the empire, who they thought of as uncivilized.

- **Barbarian** people rarely lived in large towns. Instead they lived in forts or small farming villages.

- **Many were brave warriors** but many too were skilled craftsmen, poets and humble farmers.

- **The Romans** thought barbarians wild and crude, but they survived and built a lasting civilization as the peoples of northern and western Europe.

- **They seemed** ill-disciplined in battle to the Romans, but rode horses and appeared in vast, wild, terrifying hordes.

- **The Goths** were German peoples who overran the western Roman empire in the 4th and 5th centuries. They were divided into Ostrogoths in the east near the Black Sea and Visigoths on the Danube. It was the Visigoths who under their king Alaric finally broke Rome in 476.

- **Italians later** used the term *gothic* to sneer at what they saw as the ugly cathedrals of northern Europe and the term stuck.

- **The Vandals** were a German tribe who arrived in Europe from the east in the 1st century BC. When driven west by the Huns in c.380, they took over Spain and North Africa.

- **Vandals** swept down through Italy in 455 to sack Rome and gave us the word 'vandal'.

- **The Huns** were nomadic Mongols from eastern Asia who arrived in Europe c.370, driving everyone before them, until finally defeated in 455. The Huns were bogeymen for Romans. One Roman said, 'They have a sort of shapeless lump, not a face, and pinholes for eyes' – perhaps because Huns bandaged children's skulls to deform as they grew. The most feared Hun was Attila.

Roman Britain

- **The Roman occupation** began in earnest when the armies of Claudius landed at Richborough in Kent in AD43. All of England and Wales was conquered by AD78.
- **Scotland** remained beyond Roman control. In 122-130 the 118-km-long stone wall now called Hadrian's wall was built right across the country to act as a frontier.
- **The Roman army** in Britain was powerful. There were three legions (5,000 men each) at York, Chester and Caerleon, plus 40,000 auxiliaries.
- **Roman Britain** was ruled by a Roman governor, but the Romans co-opted local chiefs to help.
- **The Romans** built the first proper towns in Britain – like St Albans, Gloucester and Lincoln – with typical Roman features such as baths and theatres.
- **Demand** for food and leather from the army and the new towns boosted farming. Large estates centred on Roman-style villas grew rich, but even small farmers did well.
- **Most people** were bilingual, speaking and writing both Celtic and Latin, and many adopted Roman lifestyles.
- **When barbarians** attacked the empire on the continent in the 300s, Roman Britain was left to fend for itself. Power fell into the hands of tyrants like the British king Vortigern (425-250).
- **Vortigern** invited Anglo-Saxons from Germany to settle in the east to help him against rebel Britons. But the Anglo-Saxons soon turned against him and invited in others of their kind to join them.
- **Villas** and towns were abandoned and Britons fled west or abroad as the Anglo-Saxons moved in.

◄ *King Arthur became the greatest hero in British legend, but the real Arthur was probably a British chief who, for a while, turned the tide against the Anglo-Saxons with a victory at Mt Badon in 500.*

Mohammed

> ★ STAR FACT ★
> The Muslim year begins with the day of Mohammed's escape to Medina, called the *Hegira*.

- **Mohammed** (c.570-632) was the Arab prophet whose teachings form the basis of the Islamic religion.
- **Muslims** believe Mohammed was the last and greatest prophet of God, who they called Allah.
- **Mohammed** was born in Mecca in Arabia.
- **His father** died before he was born and his mother died when he was a child. He was brought up by his grandfather and uncle, tending sheep and camels.
- **At the age of 25,** Mohammed entered the service of a rich widow of 40 called Khadjia and later married her. They had two sons and four daughters.
- **When 35** Mohammed was asked to restore a sacred stone damaged in a flood. A vision told him to become a prophet and proclaim the word of God.
- **The people of Mecca** resented Mohammed's preaching, and in 622 he fled to Medina.
- **In Medina** he attracted many followers. The Meccans went to war on Medina, but were driven back.
- **In 630** Mohammed re-entered Mecca in triumph, pardoned the people and set up a mosque there.

▼ *The Koran is Islam's holy book of Mohammed's teachings.*

What people wore

◄ Egyptians wore clothes made mainly of white linen. At first, men wore a short kilt, but later they wore long, wrap-around skirts. Egyptian women at first wore sheath-like dresses. After 1500BC, men and women both wore loose robes like these made from rectangles of cloth instead.

▼ Roman clothing was quite similar to the Greeks'. Men and women wore tunics, called stola (women) or tunica (men). Citizens of Rome were allowed to wear a carefully draped cloth called a toga over their tunic.

◄ Greek clothes were very simple – essentially just pieces of wool or linen wrapped round to make a tunic, dress or cloak. Young Greek men typically wore a short cloak called a chlamys over a tunic sewn up at the side and fastened at the shoulder. Women wore a dress called a chiton, made from a rectangle of cloth. They wore a longer cloak called a himation.

▶ In the north of Europe, Celtic peoples wore warm clothes made mainly of dyed wool and leather. Women wore thick dresses and headscarfs. Men wore long tunics, leggings and a cloak.

- **The earliest people** wore animal skins to keep warm.

- **The oldest signs** of woven cloth are marks in clay at Pavlov in Czechoslovakia, which date back 26,000 years.

- **Most of our knowledge** of ancient costumes comes from vases, statues and wall paintings. Colours have often faded, but we know from paintings such as those in the Roman city of Pompeii, preserved under volcanic ash, that ancient clothes were often colourful.

- **The oldest surviving clothes** come from Egyptian tombs dating back 5,000 years.

- **The deep blue** dye indigo, from the indigo plant, has been found in Egyptian cloth from 4,400 years ago.

- **Tyrian purple** was a purple dye, much-prized in ancient times. It came from Tyre (modern Lebanon) and was made from the *Purpura* and *Murex* snails.

- **People such as** the Ancient Egyptians often wore simple sandals or shoes of papyrus or leather. But the Greek dramatist Aeschylus is said to have invented the platform shoe, with 8-cm heels.

- **Minoan women** of 3,500 years ago, unusually for ancient times, wore tight-waisted dresses. Their breasts were also left exposed.

- **Ordinary Roman citizens** wore an unbleached white toga. Coloured borders showed a particular status. Public officials at functions had togas with purple borders, called a *toga praetexta*. Early Roman generals wore togas dyed in Tyrian purple. From the time of Augustus, only the emperor wore a purple toga.

Monks and monasteries

- **In religions** like Christianity and Buddhism, some devout people step out of ordinary life and live in a monastery, a community devoted entirely to religion.

- **The earliest Christian** monastery was that of the hermit St Anthony of Thebes, who went to live in the Egyptian desert about 271, and attracted followers.

- **Basil the Great** (c.329-379) and his sister Macrina the Younger founded monasteries for men and women on their estate in Cappadocia in Turkey.

- **Monasticism** spread rapidly throughout the Byzantine Empire between the 4th and 7th centuries.

- **In the West,** monasticism grew more slowly, so St Martin of Tours (316-397) sent out monks to start new communities. They were very successful in Britain and Ireland.

- **British and Irish** monasteries such as Lindisfarne and Malmesbury were centres of learning in the Dark Ages.

- **The most famous** scholar monk was St Bede of Jarrow (c.672-735), known for his history of the English people.

▶ British and Irish monks laboured to create beautiful illustrated books by hand. This is the Lindisfarne Gospel.

- **The most famous** British monastery was the Scottish Isle of Iona, set up by St Columba in 563.

- **St Benedict** (c.480-547) developed a particular way of living for monks at Monte Cassino in Italy. By 1000, most monasteries followed Benedictine rules.

- **Monasteries** were very vulnerable to Viking raids. Monks were often killed and many treasures lost, and so the monastic life lost some of its attraction.

The spread of Islam

- **Muslims** believe that their religion began the day a prophet named Mohammed left Mecca in AD622, but it was after his death in 632 that it really began to grow.

- **The spread of Islam** was led by caliphs (which means rightly guided).

- **Islam** expanded by conquest, and many peoples only became Muslims after they were conquered. But Muslim conquerors were tolerant of other religions.

- **The Muslims** regarded a conquest as a *jihad* (holy war) and this gave them a powerful zeal.

- **The Muslim Arabs** conquered Iraq (637), Syria (640), Egypt (641) and Persia (650).

- **By 661,** the Islamic Empire stretched from Tunisia to India. Its capital was Damascus.

- **The first Muslims** were Arabs, and as Islam spread, so did Arabs, but the empire contained many peoples.

- **Mohammed** commanded men to 'seek knowledge, even as far as China'. Many Muslims became great scholars.

- **Arts and sciences** flourished under Islam to make it the most cultured, advanced society in the world.

▼ The Dome of the Rock in Jerusalem, built by Abd al-Malik, was one of the first of many beautiful buildings created by Muslims.

★ STAR FACT ★
In just 100 years, the empire of Islam became bigger than the Roman Empire at its height.

The Fujiwaras

▲ *Life at the Fujiwara court was very cultured, with lots of poetry and music. But it was very formal too, with rules for everything.*

- **The Fujiwaras** were the family who dominated Japan for five centuries from the 7th century.

- **The Fujiwaras' power** really began in 858, when Fujiwara Yoshifusa married the old emperor. When he died, Yoshifusa became regent to their young son.

- **The Fujiwaras** kept their position by marrying more daughters to emperors, and creating the role of all-powerful *kampaku* (chancellor).

- **The Fujiwara** *kampaku* or regent ran the country while the emperor dealt with religious matters.

- **Fujiwara power** peaked with Michinaga (966-1028).

- **Michinaga's mansions** were more splendid than palaces and filled with banquets, concerts, poetry and picnics.

- **Many women were** novelists and poets, and love affairs were conducted via cleverly poetic letters.

- **The brilliant** court life of Michinaga was captured in the famous novel *The Tale of Genji* by the lady Murasaki.

- **During Michinaga's** reign, warrior families gained the upper hand by quelling rural rebellions, so bringing about the Fujiwaras' downfall.

> **★ STAR FACT ★**
> Sei Shonagon, a lady at Michinaga's court, wrote a famous *Pillow Book* – a diary about what she saw.

Anglo-Saxons

- **The Angles, Saxons** and Jutes were peoples from Denmark and Germany who invaded Britain and settled there between AD45 and 600.

- **The Britons resisted** at first, but by 650, they were driven back into the west or made slaves.

- **The Angles** settled in East Anglia and the Midlands, the Saxons in Sussex, Essex and Wessex (Dorset and Hampshire).

◀ *In 1939, the burial ship of the overlord Raedwald (died 625) was discovered at Sutton Hoo in East Anglia. This helmet is one of the treasures it held.*

- **Each tribe** had its own kingdom, yet by 700 most people in the south thought of themselves as English.

- **Seven leading kingdoms** formed a heptarchy: Essex, Kent, Sussex, Wessex, East Anglia, Mercia and Northumbria.

- **One king** was *bretwalda* (overlord), but the kingdoms vied for power.

- **When Ethelbert of Kent** was *bretwalda*, in 597, St Augustine converted him to Christianity. Christianity spread rapidly throughout England. English monasteries became the universities of Europe. Masons from Gaul and Rome built stone churches.

- **Some Anglo-Saxons** were farmers. Others were warriors as their famous epic poem of heroism, *Beowulf*, shows.

- **In the 700s, Danish raiders** conquered all of England but Wessex. They were pushed back by King Alfred, but attacks resumed in the reign of Ethelred II (978-1016).

- **The last Anglo-Saxon king** was Ethelred II's son, Edward the Confessor (1042-1066).

Bulgars

▶ In the 800s, the Bulgars were converted to Christianity and adopted the Eastern Orthodox church of the Byzantines. They began to create icons like this.

- **The Bulgars** were an Asian people who arrived in Europe on the Volga River c.AD370.

- **The Bulgars** were skilled horse warriors ruled by *khans* (chiefs) and *boyars* (noblemen).

- **The Bulgars** attacked the fringes of the Byzantine Empire until they were in turn attacked by another Asian people called the Avars.

- **After Kurt** became the Bulgar Khan in 605, the Bulgars re-established themselves on the steppes, but when Kurt died, the Bulgars split into five hordes.

- **Four of the five** Bulgar hordes vanished from history, but the fifth was led by Asparukh Khan, west into the Danube valley. Here they overpowered the Slavs living there to create a Bulgarian Empire.

- **Bulgarian Khans** were called caesars or czars after helping Byzantine Emperor Justinian II in 710.

- **The Bulgars** were more often at odds with the Byzantines. They were usually beaten, but after one victory, Krum Khan (803-814) lined Byzantine Emperor Nicephorus's skull with silver to make a drinking cup.

- **The Byzantines** sent St Cyril and his brother St Methodius to convert the Bulgars to Christianity. They succeeded when Czar Boris I was baptized in 864.

- **St Cyril** invented the Cyrillic alphabet, used by Russians and other eastern Europeans today.

- **The Bulgarian Empire** peaked under Simeon I (893-927). Its capital, Preslav, matched Constantinople in splendour.

The caliphs

- **The caliphs** were the rulers of Islam. The word caliph means 'successor', and they were all meant to be successors of Mohammed after he died in 632.

- **The first caliph** was Mohammed's father-in-law, Abu Bakr. After that came Umar, Uthman and Ali.

- **The first four caliphs** are called the Rashidun ('perfect') because they were the only caliphs accepted by everyone.

- **When Ali died,** in 661, Islam was torn apart by civil war. Some Muslims, called Shi'ites, saw only Ali's successors, the imams, as leaders. Most Muslims followed the Umayyad family, who became caliphs in Damascus.

- **The 14 Umayyad caliphs** expanded the Islamic Empire by conquest through North Africa and into Spain. But it proved too much for them to handle.

- **In 750** the last Umayyad caliph, Marwan II, was beaten at the Battle of the Great Zab by the rival Abbasids, who were descended from Mohammed's uncle.

- **The 38 Abbasid caliphs** turned their eyes eastwards and made a new capital at Baghdad, which soon became the richest city in the world.

- **Under the Abbasids,** Islam became famous for its science, learning and art, especially during the time of Harun al-Rashid.

- **One Umayyad** escaped to set up a rival caliphate in Spain (756-1031).

- **Descendants** of Mohammed's daughter Fatimah became caliphs in Egypt, creating the great city of Cairo.

▶ Under the Abbasid caliphs, Islamic artists made strikingly beautiful ceramic tiles and glassware.

Alfred the Great

- **Alfred the Great** (AD849-899) was the greatest of the Anglo-Saxon kings.

- **Alfred** became king of Wessex in 871 at a time when the Danes had over-run East Anglia, Northumbria and Mercia.

- **In 878,** a series of ferocious Danish attacks drove Alfred to hide on the isle of Athelney in the Somerset marshes.

- **While on the run,** Alfred is said to have hidden in a pigherd's cottage. He was so tired he fell asleep by the fire, letting some cakes burn. Not realizing he was the king, the pigherd's wife scolded him.

- **From Athelney,** Alfred secretly assembled an army and emerged to score a decisive victory over the

> ★ STAR FACT ★
> Alfred translated many books from Latin into English so that his people could read them.

◀ This enamel and gold brooch was found near Athelney. It is inscribed with the words Aelfred me ech eh t gewyrcan – Old English for 'Alfred ordered me to be made'.

Danes at Edington. The Danes agreed to withdraw to East Anglia and their king Guthrum became a Christian.

- **In 886,** Alfred recaptured London and forced the Danes to stay within an area called Danelaw.

- **Alfred built forts,** reorganized his army and also created England's first navy to defend against invasions.

- **Alfred was a** wise and kindly king who created sound laws, protected the weak from corrupt judges and created laws to help the poor and needy.

- **Alfred was a scholar** who encouraged learning. He decreed that all young men should learn to read English, and made important books available in English.

The Berbers

- **The Berbers** were the people who lived in North Africa before other peoples arrived.

- **'Berber'** comes from *barbara*, Roman for barbarians.

- **Numidian Berbers** allied themselves with Carthage (in what is now Tunisia), the city created when Phoenician traders from Lebanon settled here 3,000 years ago.

- **The Berbers** lived with first Carthaginian, then Roman, Vandal and Byzantine invasions by withdrawing south into the desert, staying as bands of marauders.

- **In the 7th century,** Islamic Arabs invaded North Africa and many Berbers became Muslims.

- **The Berbers** kept their independence by changing Islam to their own tastes. They based their religion on marabouts, holy men who lived very frugally and morally.

- **After 740,** Berbers took back control of North Africa from the Umayyad caliphs.

- **The Berbers** built empires extending into Spain under the Almohads (1121-1269) and Almoravids (1061-1145).

- **Ibn Tumart** was the first Almohad leader, from c.1121. He claimed to be the Mahdi, the holy man whose coming was predicted by Mohammed.

- **The Berber empires** fell to the Arabs in the 12th century.

◀ When their empires fell, Berbers survived out in the Sahara desert.

The Vikings

- **The Vikings** were daring raiders from Norway, Sweden and Denmark. Between AD800 and 1100, they swept in on the coasts of northwest Europe in their longships, searching for rich plunder to carry away.

- **People** were terrified by the lightning raids of the Vikings. A prayer of the time went, 'Deliver us, O Lord, from the fury of the Norsemen (Vikings). They ravage our lands. They kill our women and children.'

- **Vikings** prided themselves on their bravery in battle. Most fought on foot with swords, spears and axes. Rich Vikings rode on horseback.

- **Shock troops** called *berserkers* led the attack. *Berserk* is Norse for 'bare shirt' as they wore no armour. Before a battle, they became fighting mad through drink and drugs and trusted in their god Odin to keep them safe.

- **The word** 'Viking' was only used later. People of the time called them Norsemen. The word probably came from *Vik*, a pirate centre in Norway. When Norsemen went 'a-viking', they meant fighting as a pirate. Swedish Vikings who settled in eastern Europe may have been called *Rus*, and so Russia was named after them.

- **Not all Vikings** were pirates. At home, they were farmers and fishermen, merchants and craftworkers. Many went with the raiders and settled in the north of France, in northern England and in Dublin.

- ▶ The main Viking gods were Odin, Thor and Frey. The Anglo-Saxons had the same gods and their names have given us some days of the week: Odin's or Wodin's day (Wednesday), Thor's day (Thursday) and Frey's or Frigg's day (Friday). Thor's symbol was a hammer called Mjollnir, which caused thunder and lightning. A hammer like this one was used at many stages in a Viking's life – raised over the newborn, laid in the bride's lap at weddings, or carved on a gravestone.

- **The Vikings attacked** mainly Britain and Ireland, but raided as far as Gibraltar and into the Mediterranean.

- **In Eastern Europe,** the Vikings' ships carried them inland up various rivers. They ventured far through Russia and the Ukraine, sometimes marauding as far south as Constantinople, which they called 'Miklagard', the big city.

- **The Norsemen** who settled in northern France were called Normans. The Norman king William the Conqueror, who invaded England in 1066, was descended from their leader, Rollo.

> ★ STAR FACT ★
> In November 885, Count Odo and 200 knights fought heroically to defend Paris against Viking hordes but the city was reduced to ashes.

▼ The Vikings were master sailors, and their wooden sailing ships, called longships, are masterpieces of boat-building – light and flat-bottomed enough to sail up shallow rivers, yet seaworthy in the open ocean.

The ships often had a high prow, sometimes carved with a dragon's head

Shields were strapped in rows down each side

When the wind was still, they relied on banks of 20-30 rowers each side

At sea, ships were driven along by a large, square sail made from strips of woollen cloth stitched together

The ships were steered with a large paddle at the rear

The first Russians

- **Little is known** of the earliest days of Russia, because it was inhabited mainly by nomadic peoples who left few records – such as the Cimmerians (1200-700BC) and later Huns and Khazars.

- **In the 800s AD,** Russia was on the major trade route from NW Europe to the world's richest cities – Constantinople and Baghdad.

- **Slavic peoples** set up trading towns such as Novgorod. They traded in amber, furs, honey, wax and wood.

- **From around 860,** Viking adventurers raided and traded in the region. They were known as the Varangian Rus. The most famous of them was Rurik of Jutland, who took over Novgorod.

- **The city of Kiev** grew up further south, on the Dnieper River.

◀ Kiev, in the Ukraine, was the focus of the first Russian nation, from 900-1100.

- **Soon** the Varangian 'grand prince' of Kiev ruled over a vast area historians call Kievan Rus. This covered what is now the Ukraine and eastern Russia.

- **In c.970,** the Slavs took over Kiev under Prince Svyatoslav and his son Vladimir.

- **Vladimir** made Kievan Rus the first Russian nation.

- **Legend says** Vladimir sent people to study different religions. Nothing impressed them until they reached the Hagia Sophia in Constantinople. They were so stunned 'they knew not whether they were in heaven or on earth'.

- **Kiev** quickly adopted Byzantine Christianity. Within 50 years it had 200 beautiful churches – including its own Hagia Sophia – and Vladimir was Russia's first saint.

Harun al-Rashid

- **Harun al-Rashid** (766-809) was the most famous of all the caliphs.

- **In Harun's time**, Baghdad became the most glamorous city in the world, famed for its luxury as well as its poetry, music and learning.

- **Harun** was famous far and wide. He sent ambassadors to the Chinese emperor and an elephant to Charlemagne.

- **Harun's wife** Zubaydah would only drink from silver and gold cups studded with gems.

◀ The magic and romance of Harun's Baghdad is captured in the tales of The Arabian Nights.

- **Harun** was a great patron of the arts, and gave lavish gifts to poets and musicians. Yet he also enjoyed watching dogs fight – and often had people executed.

- **Stories tell** how Harun would wander in the moonlight with his friend Abu Nuwas, the brilliant poet, as well as Masrur the executioner.

- **Harun** has become famous because he features in the famous collection of 200-odd tales of *The Thousand and One Nights*, or *The Arabian Nights*.

- *The Arabian Nights* includes such famous characters as Aladdin and his genie, Ali Baba and Sinbad the Sailor.

- **The tales** begin with King Shahriyar of Samarkand distraught by his wife's unfaithfulness. He vows to marry a new girl each night and behead her in the morning.

- **The lovely princess Scheherazade** insists on marrying the king, then at night tells him a tale so entertaining that he lets her live another day to finish it. One story leads to another for 1001 nights, by which time the king has fallen completely in love with her.

The Holy Roman Empire

- **The Holy Roman Empire** was a mostly German empire that lasted from 800 until 1806.

- **It began** when Pope Leo III tried to gain the protection of Charlemagne, the King of the Franks, by reviving the idea of the Roman Empire.

- **Pope Leo III** is said to have taken Charlemagne by surprise in St Peter's church in Rome on Christmas Day 800, and to have placed the crown on his head.

- **Charlemagne's Frankish Empire**, including France, Germany and Italy, became the Holy Roman Empire.

- **When Charlemagne died,** in 814, the newborn Holy Roman Empire fell apart.

- **150 years later,** in 962, the German King Otto I gained control of Italy as well as Germany and insisted the pope crown him Holy Roman Emperor.

- **Over the centuries** the empire was continually beset by conflicts with both powerful Germans and the pope.

- **In 1076,** Pope Gregory VII and Emperor Henry IV were

▲ Until 1531, all Holy Roman Emperors were crowned at Aachen in Germany, where Charlemagne built a cathedral and lies buried.

vying for control. Henry's subjects sided with the pope, so Henry had to give way.

- **Gregory** forced Henry to stand barefoot in snow for three days outside his castle in Tuscany to beg for a pardon.

- **The pope's Vatican** and other Italian cities gained almost complete independence from the emperor.

The Toltecs

> ★ STAR FACT ★
> The name *Toltec* has many meanings: 'cultured person', 'city-type' and 'reed people'.

- **By 900,** the city of Teotihuacán was destroyed and much of Mexico was in the hands of warrior tribes from the north.

- **Legend says** that Teotihuacán was destroyed by one of these warrior tribes called the Toltecs, led by their ruler Mixcóatl. *Mixcóatl* means 'Cloud Serpent'.

- **Under Mixcóatl's son,** Topiltzin, the Toltec were said to have built an empire and also a capital at Tollan, now thought to be Tula, 45 km north of Mexico City.

- **Topiltzin** introduced the cult of the god *Quetzalcóatl* ('Feathered Serpent'), and took the name himself.

- **The Toltecs** were not only great warriors but fine builders and craftsmen. Tollan was full of pyramids, temples and other huge, impressive buildings.

- **Legend says** Tolpiltzin Quetzalcóatl was driven out of Tollan by jealous rivals – including the priests of the god Tezcatlipoca ('Smoking Mirror').

- **After leaving Tollan,** Quetzalcóatl sailed east into the Gulf of Mexico, vowing to return one day.

- **The Aztecs** were greatly influenced by the Toltecs. The Aztecs got the idea of human sacrifices from the priests of Tezcatlipoca. Some Aztecs believed that, when the Spanish arrived in 1519, it was Quetzalcóatl returning in vengeance.

- **The Toltec Empire** broke up in the 12th century and Tollan vanished.

▶ Toltec temples in Tollan were guarded by stone statues of warriors such as this.

The Maoris

▲ The Maoris lived mostly near the coast or by rivers and travelled in light, swift canoes.

- **The early Polynesian** settlers came to New Zealand by canoe from islands in the Pacific.

- **In c.AD100,** Polynesians called the Morioris came here to settle from the Cook, Marquesas or Society Islands.

- **Maori** tradition tells how the Maoris arrived in waves of migration, beginning about 1150 and ending with the coming of a great fleet from the mythical land of Hawaiki 200 years later.

- **Hawaiki** is thought to be the Pacific island of Tahiti.

- **Archaeologists** have found signs of Maori settlement in New Zealand dating back to AD800 and earlier.

- **The first Maoris** lived mainly by hunting and fishing.

- **Maoris** were skilled woodworkers, building beautiful wooden houses covered in carvings.

- **No human** set foot on New Zealand before around 2,000 years ago.

- **The first settlers** in New Zealand were Polynesians.

> ★ STAR FACT ★
> The first Maoris hunted gigantic, flightless birds called moas, which are now extinct.

Charlemagne

- **In 732,** the Frankish (early French) leader Charles Martel halted the great Muslim invasion of Europe in battle at Tours in central France.

- **Martel's** son Pepin the Short made sure of his family's hold on power in the Frankish kingdom. In 768, Pepin's son Charlemagne became King of the Franks.

- **Charlemagne** (742-814) was the greatest European ruler for 1,000 years after Rome's fall.

- **Charlemagne's** name means Charles the Great.

- **Charlemagne** was a great military leader, taking his armies on 53 successful campaigns. He scored victories against the Moors in Spain, and against Saxons and Avars in central Europe.

- **By 796,** Charlemagne had created an empire joining France, Germany, northern Italy and northern Spain.

- **Charlemagne** was a Christian, and in AD800 the pope made Charlemagne Holy Roman Emperor.

- **Charlemagne** was a great ruler who set up an effective law system and introduced the idea of juries in trials.

- **Charlemagne** knew Latin, German and Greek and encouraged scholarship, helped by the great teacher Alcuin.

- **The palace school** in Charlemagne's capital Aachen was the most important school in Europe.

◄ After his death, many legends grew up about Charlemagne. We know that he must have been a powerful personality. One eyewitness said: 'He had a broad and strong body of unusual height...and strode with a firm step and held himself like a man.'

The Magyars

- **The plains** by the River Danube (an area now in Hungary) were settled early in the history of humankind, but little is known of the area before it formed the Roman provinces Dacia and Pannonia. At this time, it was home to Celts and Slavs.

- **Roman Dacia and Pannonia** fell early to the barbarian invaders – Goths, Huns and Avars.

- **In 796,** the Avars were crushed by Charlemagne.

- **In 892,** another Frankish king called Arnulf asked a people called the Magyars to help him against the Moravians, who now lived on the Danube plain.

- **The Magyars** were a people who lived from 3000BC to 800 on the steppes near Russia's River Don.

- **In 889,** the Magyars had been driven to the edge of their land by a people called the Pechenegs, so they were grateful for Arnulf's call.

- **Led by the legendary Arpad,** the Magyars swept into Hungary and made it their home.

- **In 975,** Arpad's great-grandson Géza became a Christian and began to form the Magyars into the Hungarian nation.

- **Géza's son** Stephen (997-1038) carried on his work and became the first king of Hungary.

- **King Stephen,** also called St Stephen, was crowned by the pope on Christmas Day, AD1000.

▲ King Stephen is a famous figure in Hungarian history and his crown became the symbol of the nation.

Viking voyages

- **The Vikings** were great seafarers who made some of the most remarkable voyages of ancient times.

- **The Vikings sailed** east through the Baltic and up the Vistula and Dnieper Rivers.

- **The Vikings** sailed west around the British Isles, south round Spain into the Mediterranean.

- **The most daring** Viking voyages were out across the then-unknown open ocean of the North Atlantic.

- **From 900,** the Vikings sailed to and settled on remote islands to the far north – including Iceland, the Faroes and Greenland.

▶ This map shows just some of the remarkable voyages made by the Vikings, and their approximate dates. Names in brackets are the Viking names.

- **About 800,** Vikings led by Ohthere reached the remote Siberian islands of Novaya Zemlya in the Arctic.

- **In 1000,** Bjarni Herjulffson was blown off course sailing home from Greenland and saw an unknown shore.

- **Leif Eriksson** sailed west to find this unknown shore. Sagas tell how he found a new land. The Vikings called it Vinland because it was said to be abundant in 'wine berries'. The wine berries he found were probably cranberries.

- **Most experts** now think Vinland is North America, and Leif was the first European to reach it.

- **In AD1004,** the Viking Thorfinn took 130 people to settle in Vinland and stayed three years. Remains of Thorfinn's settlement were found in 1963 at L'Anse aux Meadows, on the northern tip of Newfoundland.

Famous villains

- **Ancient history** has many famous villains – but most were called villains by their enemies, so we can never be sure just how bad they were.

- **Many of the best-known** villains are Roman, including the Emperors Caligula and Nero and Sejanus, Emperor Tiberius's minister, who is believed to have poisoned Drusus, Tiberius's son.

- **The Emperor Claudius's wife** Messalina (AD22-48) got Claudius to execute any man who resisted her advances. She once made love to hundreds of men in a night.

- **Claudius's fourth wife,** his niece Agrippina (AD15-59), probably poisoned him to make way for her son, Nero.

- **Many stories** are told of the Chinese emperor Shi Huangdi's cruelty, including killing 460 scholars.

- **Artaxerxes** (died 338BC) was the cruel Persian king who ravaged Egypt in 343BC.

- **Artaxerxes** and all his sons but Arses were murdered by his minister Bagoas in 338BC. Bagoas then killed Arses and tried to poison the next king, Darius III. Darius found out and made Bagoas drink the poison himself.

- **Herod the Great** (73BC-4BC) of Judea (modern Israel) was a strong king, but he is known best for the murder of his beloved wife Mariamne in a jealous rage and the Biblical tale of the Slaughter of the Innocents. This tale relates how Herod ordered soldiers to kill all babies in Bethlehem in order to get rid of the infant Jews, who prophets had said would be a threat to him.

- **Pontius Pilate** (AD36) was the Roman governor of Judea who let Jesus be crucified.

- **Theodora** was notorious for her secret police.

◄ History paints Nero (top) and Caligula (left) as real villains.

Viking society

- **Vikings ate** beef, cheese, eggs and milk from their farms, meat from deer, elks and seals caught by hunters and fish such as cod, herring and salmon.

- **Vikings lived** in one-storey wooden houses with slanted roofs of turf or straw and no windows. At the centre was a hearth for warmth and cooking. The man of the house sat on a chair called the high seat; the rest sat on benches.

◄ Viking god Odin was said to ride on the eight-legged horse Sleipnir, accompanied by two ravens that brought him news of any battles.

> ★ STAR FACT ★
> Viking villages were ruled by a council called the *Thing* or *Folkmoot*.

- **Viking men wore** trousers and a long-sleeved smock shirt. Women wore long woollen or linen dresses.

- **Viking men** could have two or three wives, but marriages were arranged by parents.

- **A Viking woman,** unusually for the time, could own her own property and divorce her husband.

- *Skalds* (poets) went into battle to report on them in verse.

- **The Vikings** were great storytellers. They told of their adventures in long stories called *sagas*.

- **At first** the sagas were only spoken. From 1100-1300, they were written. The most famous is *Njal's saga*.

- **Vikings** were very religious and had several gods. They believed if they died fighting they would go to Valhalla, a special hall in Asgard, the gods' home.

The first English kings

- **Egbert,** king of Wessex from 802 to 839, became in effect the first king of England when he conquered Mercia at Ellandun in 829. But his rule lasted just a year before the Mercian king Wiglaf claimed Mercia back.

- **For 100 years,** much of England was lost to the Danes, but Alfred the Great's son Edward and his daughter Aethelflaed gradually drove the Danes out by 918.

◀ The city of Winchester in southern England was Alfred the Great's capital, and in his time it became a great centre of learning. Canute also made it his capital, and his son Hardecanute is buried here, with Alfred.

- **England's kingship** really began with Athelstan, who was crowned 'king of all Britain' at Kingston on 4 Sept., 925.

- **Ethelred the Unready** was king of England from 978-1013 and 1014-1016. *Rede* was old English for advice, and his name meant he was always badly advised.

- **Ethelred** created so much distrust among his subjects that the Danes easily re-conquered England in 980.

- **In 1013** Dane Sweyn Forkbeard became king of England.

- **When Sweyn** died, Ethelred made a comeback until Sweyn's son Canute drove him out. Canute became king of England in 1016 by marrying Ethelred's widow, Emma.

- **Canute** ruled well. A story tells how he rebuked flatterers by showing how even he could not stop the tide coming in.

- **After Canute,** in 1035, came his son Hardecanute, who died in 1042. Ethelred's son Edward the Confessor then became king – but the Danes did not want a Saxon king.

- **The Danes** called on their Norwegian allies, led first by Magnus then Harold Hardraada, to win back the throne.

Early Scots

- **The first settlers** came to Scotland around 7,000 years ago, and the remains of their huts can be seen on Skara Brae in Orkney.

- **People called Picts** arrived here shortly before the times of the Romans, who failed to conquer Scotland.

- **The Picts** may have come from the Black Sea region. They got their name from the tattooed pictures on their bodies.

- **Brochs** are 15-m high stone towers built for defence around 100BC – perhaps by ancestors of the Picts.

- **Celts** called Scots came from Dalriada in Ireland in c.470. They soon conquered the west.

- **After St Columba** came to set up Iona monastery in 563, Scotland was slowly converted to Christianity.

- **In 563** Scotland was split into four kingdoms: the Scots' Dalriada in the west; the Picts in the north; the Britons' Strathclyde in the southwest; and Bernicia or Lothian of the Angles in the east.

- **In 685,** the Picts drove out the Angles, and in 863, the Dalriada king Kenneth McAlpin conquered the Picts to create a country called Alba, the first Scotland.

- **In the 900s and 1000s,** many people fought to be king in Scotland. Kenneth III killed Constantine III to become king. Malcolm II killed Kenneth III and Duncan I who followed him was killed by his general Macbeth. Macbeth was killed by Malcolm III.

- **Malcolm III's** wife was Saint Margaret (1045-1093), brought up in Hungary where her father was in exile.

▶ Macbeth (died 1057) was the Scottish king who became the basis for Shakespeare's tragedy 'Macbeth'. The real Macbeth killed Duncan in battle, not in his bed as in Shakespeare's play.

1000 THINGS
YOU SHOULD KNOW ABOUT

MODERN
HISTORY

KEY

People

The Americas

Wars and battles

Events

Europe

The World

The Norman invasion

- **On 5 January 1066,** the English king Edward the Confessor died. As he died, he named as his successor Harold Godwin – the powerful earl of the kingdom of Wessex.

- **Harold's claim** to the English throne was challenged by William, the duke of Normandy in France, who claimed that Edward had already promised him the throne.

- **Harold's claim** was also challenged by Harold Hardraade (the Ruthless), the king of Norway.

- **In autumn 1066,** Hardraade invaded northern England with Harold Godwin's brother Tostig. His army was routed by Harold's at Stamford Bridge on 25 September.

- **On 27 Sept,** William's Norman army of 7,000 crossed from France and landed at Pevensey in S. England.

- ◄ The Normans commemorated their victory at the Battle of Hastings with a famous tapestry, now in Bayeux in France.

- **Harold marched** his army south to meet the Normans, walking over 300 km to London in just five days.

- **Harold's tired army** met the Normans at Hastings in Sussex on the 14th October, and took a stand by the Hoar Apple Tree on Caldbec Hill.

- **Harold's army** was mauled by William's archers, but axe-wielding English house-carles (infantry) put the Norman cavalry to flight. Harold was then killed – perhaps by an arrow. The English fought on for a while before fleeing.

- **After the battle** William moved on London, where he was crowned king in Westminster Abbey on 25 December.

- **Within** a few years, the Normans had conquered England.

The great khans

- **The Mongols** were nomads who lived in yurts (huts made of felt) in central Asia, as many still do .

- **In 1180,** a 13-year-old Mongol boy called Temujin was made khan (chief) of his tribe. He soon became a great leader, and in 1206 he was hailed as *Genghis Khan* (Chief of all Men).

- **Genghis Khan** was a brilliant and ruthless soldier. His armies terrified their enemies, and butchered anyone they met.

- ◄ *Genghis Khan was a man of incredible physical strength and willpower. He could be tyrannical and cruel, yet philosophers would travel from far away to talk with him about religion.*

- **Genghis's horse archers** could kill at 180 m while riding at full gallop. They once rode 440 km in just three days.

- **In just four years (1210-14),** Genghis Khan conquered northern China, much of India and Persia. His empire stretched right through Asia from Korea to the Caspian.

- **After Genghis Khan** died, his son Ogodai ravaged Armenia, Hungary and Poland.

- **Genghis Khan's grandson** – Kublai Khan – conquered the rest of China in 1265 and made himself the first of a line of Mongol emperors of China called Yuans. The Yuans lasted until 1368.

- **Kublai's** rule in China was harsh, but he was greatly admired by the Venetian traveller, Marco Polo.

- **Kublai Khan** created a grand new capital called Ta-tu ('the Great Capital') – now Beijing.

- **Kublai Khan** adopted Chinese ways of government and ruled with such efficiency that China became very rich.

The Aztecs

- **In the 1200s,** a tribe called the Aztecs found that the only place to settle in crowded Mexico was on a lake.

- **By 1325,** the Aztecs were powerful and their lake home Tenochtitlán was a splendid city with canals and temples.

- **Aztec farmers** walked or rowed dugout canoes for hours to markets in cities like Tlateloco to sell farm produce in return for cocoa beans, which they used as money.

- **In Aztec society,** a powerful priest-king plus priests and nobles ruled ordinary folk and slaves with an iron hand.

- **The Aztecs** built vast pyramids topped by temples where priests made bloody human sacrifices on a huge scale.

- **The Aztecs** made human sacrifices because they believed that this gave their god Huitzilopochtli the strength to fight off the night and bring the morning.

> ★ STAR FACT ★
> Every year Tenochtitlán took in 9,000 tonnes of corn, beans and seeds in taxes.

▶ Aztec high-priests were awesome figures who made human sacrifices to the gods.

- **In a special, sacred ball game** teams hit a rubber ball through a small ring in an I-shaped court – using their hips, knees and elbows. This very violent game caused serious injury, even death.

- **One of the ways** we know about the Aztecs is from folding books of picture-writing called codices, written by Aztec scribes. The most famous is the *Codex Mendoza*.

- **By 1521,** the Aztec Empire is finished. Spanish treasure-seekers led by Hernando Cortés defeat Montezuma II the Aztec emperor, and plunder their land and riches.

The Magna Carta

- **John I** was king of England from 1199 to 1216. He was one of the most unpopular kings in history.

- **John was nicknamed** 'Lackland' by his father Henry II because, unlike his older brothers Richard and Geoffrey, he did not inherit land to provide him an income.

- **John was hated** for his cruelty, for the demands he put on his barons for tax and military service and for trying to seize the crown while his popular brother King Richard the Lionheart was crusading.

- **On 15 June 1215,** rebellious barons compelled John to meet them at Runnymede on the Thames and agree to their demands by sealing the Magna Carta ('Great Charter').

▼ The barons compelled King John to put his seal (wax stamp) on the Magna Carta at Runnymede in 1215.

- **Ordinary people** gained little at the time from the Magna Carta but it is now seen as the world's first bill of rights and the start of fair government in England.

- **The Magna Carta** showed that even the king had to obey the law.

- **Magna Carta** contained 63 clauses, most relating to feudal customs.

- **Clause 39** gave every free man the right to a fair trial. Clause 40 gave everyone the right to instant justice.

- **Some parts of** the Magna Carta dealt with weights and measures, catching fish and foreign merchants.

- **John** got the pope to annul the document three days later, but it was reissued in 1225, after John's death.

Saladin

- **Saladin** was perhaps the greatest Muslim (Islamic) leader of the Middle Ages. To his people he was a saintly hero. Even his Christian enemies were awed by his honour and bravery.

- **Saladin is famed** as a brilliant soldier, but he was also deeply religious. He built many schools, mosques and canals.

- **Saladin was a Kurd,** born in Tekrit, now in Iraq, in 1137, but he was brought up in Syria.

- **He became** a soldier at the age of 14. Right from the start he had an intense belief in the idea of *jihad* – the holy war to spread the Islamic religion.

◀ *Saladin must have been a single-minded and ambitious man, but those who met him said he was the most humble, moral and generous of rulers. Strangely, he died virtually penniless.*

- **Saladin's leadership** brought him to prominence and in 1169 he was effectively made sultan (ruler) of Egypt.

- **By diplomacy and conquest,** he united the Muslim countries – torn apart by rivalries for the 88 years since the crusaders captured Jerusalem in 1099.

- **In 1187,** with Islam united, Saladin was able to turn his attentions to driving the crusaders out of the Near East.

- **On 4 July 1187** Saladin routed the Crusaders at Hattin in Palestine. This victory was so devastating to the Crusaders that within three months the Muslims had recaptured almost every bit of land they had lost.

- **Shocked by the fall** of Jerusalem, the Christian countries threw themselves into their last major Crusade, led in part by the great Richard the Lionheart.

- **Such was Saladin's** leadership that the Muslims fought off the crusaders' onslaught. Eventually, Richard and Saladin met up and, in a spirit of mutual admiration, drew up a truce that ended the Crusades.

Bannockburn

▶ *The story goes that, while in hiding, Robert Bruce was inspired to go on fighting after seeing a spider struggle up its thread again and again – and eventually succeed.*

- **In 1286, King Alexander III** of Scotland died. His grand-daughter – Margaret – 'Maid of Norway', died four years later. Their deaths left no obvious successor to the Scottish throne.

- **The Scottish lords** agreed to the suggestion of English king Edward I that he should decide between the 13 rival claimants, including John de Balliol and Robert Bruce.

- **Edward I** marched into Scotland, imprisoned the leading claimant John de Balliol and declared himself king. Some of Balliol's rivals, such as Robert, supported Edward.

- **The Scottish lords** did not react, but a small landowner called William Wallace began a heroic fight. With a band of just 30 men, he attacked Lanark, took the garrison and killed the English sheriff. Commoners flocked to his aid.

★ **STAR FACT** ★
At Bannockburn, just 5,000 Scots may have routed an English army of 23,000.

- **On 4 May 1297,** Wallace's small rebel army scored a stunning victory over the English at Stirling. He drove the English from Scotland and marched on into England. But the Scottish lords still gave him no support.

- **Wallace** was captured by the English in 1305. He was hung, drawn (disembowelled) and quartered (cut in four pieces). His head was stuck on a pole on London Bridge.

- **Wallace's** heroism inspired Robert Bruce to lead a rebellion that finally included the Scottish lords.

- **Letting his enemies** think he was dead, Robert launched a campaign from Ireland in 1306. Within two years he had cleared the English from Scotland again.

- **Robert scored** a last decisive victory over the English under Edward II at Bannockburn on 23-24 June 1314. With this victory, the Scots regained their independence.

VA DESCRIPTIO.

African empires

- **From 1000 to 1500,** the interaction of black, Bantu-speaking Africans with Arab Muslims shaped African history.

- **In East Africa,** Bantu people and Arabs mixed to create the culture and language called Swahili.

- **Trade in gold and ivory** created thriving ports down the East African coast – such as Zanzibar and Kilwa.

- **Inland** the city of Great Zimbabwe flourished within its huge granite walls. It is now a ruin, but in the 1400s, gold made this city the heart of the Monomatapa Empire.

- **Further inland,** by the lakes of Uganda, were the extraordinary grass palaces of the Bugandan kings.

- **In West Africa,** trade across the Sahara made kingdoms like Ghana flourish. Two great empires grew up – first Mali (1240-1500) and then Songhai, which peaked in the 1500s.

- **The Mali** Empire centred on the city of Timbuktu.

- **Timbuktu's** glory began in 1324, when King Mansa Musa went on a grand trip to Mecca with camels laden with gold and brought back the best scholars and architects.

▶ This mask was made by the Edo people, who made Benin the greatest city in Africa in the 1600s.

- **Timbuktu** means 'mother with a large navel', after an old woman said to have first settled here. But from 1324-1591 Timbuktu was a splendid city with the world's biggest university, catering for 25,000 students.

- **The Songhai Empire** in the 1400s stretched right across West Africa from what is now Nigeria to Gambia. It reached its peak under Sunni Ali (1464-92), who conquered Timbuktu, and his son Askia the Great (1493-1528).

Serfs and lords

- **When the Roman** Empire collapsed, a new way of ordering society, called the feudal system, emerged.

- **In the feudal system,** a king or overlord gave a lord a *fief* (a grant of land). In return, the lord swore to train and fight for the king as a knight (horse warrior). Land was the security because it could not be moved. Any lord who got a fief was called his king's *vassal*.

- **In 732, Charles Martel,** ruler of the Franks (now France) drove back the invading Muslims at the Battle of Tours. But he was worried he might not beat the brilliant Muslim horsemen if they came back. So he developed one of the first feudal systems.

- **There were** different levels in the feudal system. The count of Champagne had 2,017 vassal knights, but he himself was vassal to ten overlords, including the king of France.

- **Only noblemen** could join the feudal system, but it soon took over most land in Europe, as kings tied their subjects by grants of land.

- **There was a saying**, 'No land without a lord; and no lord without a land'.

- **With so much land** in fiefs, most peasants were serfs, legally bound to their lords by the 'manorial' system, which centred on a lord's manor or castle.

- **Serfs** were given small plots of land to live off in return for working their lord's land.

- **Serfs** could not be evicted, but had few rights. They could not leave the village, marry or sell their possessions without their lord's permission.

- **The feudal and manorial systems** reached their peak in the 1100s but then began to decline.

◀ Most people in medieval Europe were poor serfs tied to their lord. They lived in poor huts clustered round the lord's manor house and scraped a poor living.

Crusades

- **In the 11th century,** western Christian countries were feeling very threatened by the growing empire of the Muslim Seljuk Turks. In 1095, they were just a few miles outside Constantinople, capital of the Byzantine Empire and the main centre of Christianity in the east. The Byzantine emperor Alexander Comnenus appealed to the pope, Urban II, for help.

- **Urban II** held a meeting of church leaders at Clermont in France. He called for warriors to drive back the Turks and reclaim the Holy Land from the Muslims. This was not just a battle but a holy pilgrimage or Crusade. The word 'Crusade' comes from the Latin *crux*, meaning 'cross', the Christian symbol.

- **Before the armies** could set out, 50,000 peasants began marching from western Europe on their own 'People's Crusade' to free the Holy Land. They had been stirred by tales of Turkish atrocities, spread by a preacher called Peter the Hermit. Many peasants died or got lost on the way; the rest were killed by Turks.

- **In 1096,** armies of well-trained French and Norman knights set out on the First Crusade. At Constantinople, they joined up with the Byzantines. Despite a lot of quarrelling on the way, they captured Jerusalem in 1099 and then set about massacring Jews and Turks mercilessly.

- **After capturing** Jerusalem, the crusaders divided the Holy Land into four parts or Counties, together known as Outremer (said 'oot-rer-mare') which meant 'land beyond the seas'. The crusaders ruled Outremer for 200 years and built great castles like Krak des Chevaliers in Syria.

- **Two bands of soldier-monks** formed to protect pilgrims journeying to the Holy Land – the Knights Hospitallers of St John and the Knights Templars. The Hospitallers wore black with a white cross. The Templars wore a red cross on white, which became the symbol of all crusaders.

- **By 1144,** crusader control in Outremer weakened, and the Turks advanced. King Louis VII of France and King Conrad of Germany launched a Second Crusade. But by 1187, Saladin had retaken most of Outremer.

- **In 1190,** the three most powerful men in Europe – Richard I of England, Philip II of France and Frederick Barbarossa (Holy Roman Emperor) – set off on the Third Crusade. Barbarossa died on the way and Philip II gave up. Only Richard went on, and secured a truce with Saladin.

- **In 1212,** thousands of children set off on a Children's Crusade to take back Jerusalem, led by French farm boy Stephen of Cloyes. Sadly, most were lured on to ships in Marseilles and sold into slavery or prostitution.

◄▲ When the crusader knights set out to fight in the Holy Land for Jerusalem (above), they went with different motives. Some were courageous men with a deep sense of honour and a holy purpose. Others were adventurers, out for personal gain or glory. This crusader wears the famous uniform of the Knights Templars.

Marco Polo

- **Marco Polo** was a famous Italian traveller. Born c.1254 in Venice, he spent many years in the court of Kublai Khan, emperor of China.

- **In the 1200s,** most of Europe knew China only as the romantic land of 'Cathay'. But Marco's father Niccolo and uncle Maffeo were well-travelled merchants who had already been there.

- **In 1271,** Niccolo and Maffeo invited 17-year-old Marco to come with them to Cathay again.

- **The Polos took four years** to reach China, travelling on foot and horse along the 'Silk Road' – a route north of the Himalayan mountains. The Silk Road was the way merchants brought silk from China to Europe.

- **Kublai Khan** welcomed the Polos. Marco had a gift for languages and became one of the Khan's diplomats.

Outward journey 1271-75
Return journey 1292-95

◀ Marco Polo was one of the few Europeans to journey all the way to China and back in the Middle Ages.

- **After 17 years,** the Polos decided to come back – but the Khan would only let them go if they took with them a princess who was to be wed to the Khan's grand-nephew in Persia.

- **The Polos** arrived back in Venice in 1295, laden with jewels, silks and spices.

- **Marco Polo** later wrote an account of his time in China while a prisoner of war in Genoa, dictating it to a man called Rustichello. It immediately became a best-seller.

- **Marco's** tales were so fantastic that some called the book *Il milione* ('The million lies'). Experts now think that he reported the truth as he saw it.

- **Christopher Columbus** was just one of many people inspired by Marco Polo's accounts.

The Black Death

▲ The Plague brought death so close to people that they began to think of death as a real person.

- **The Black Death** was the terrible epidemic of bubonic plague and pneumonia that ravaged Europe between 1347 and 1351.

- **The Black Death** of the 1300s was perhaps the worst disaster ever to have struck humanity.

- **Worldwide,** the Black Death killed 40 million people.

- **The Black Death** killed 25 million people in Europe.

- **The disease** probably started in China. It was transmitted to Europeans when a Kipchak (Mongol) raiding party catapulted infected corpses into a Genoese trading centre in the Crimea.

- **The plague reached Genoa** in 1347 and spread west and north, reaching London and Paris in 1348.

- **The plague was** carried first by rat fleas that could also live on humans. It then changed to pneumonic plague which was spread through coughs and sneezes.

- **After the Black Death,** fields were littered with bodies. Houses, villages and towns stood silent and empty.

- **Afterwards** there was such a shortage of labour that wages soared and many serfs gained their freedom.

> ★ STAR FACT ★
> The Black Death killed more than one in every four Europeans in just four years.

The Hundred Years' War

▲ The greatest knight of the war was Edward the Black Prince (1330-76), hero of the Battles of Crécy, Poitiers and Navarette.

- **The Hundred Years' War** was a long war between France and England, lasting from 1337 to 1453.

- **The war** was caused by disputes over Guyenne (English land in southwest France), English claims to the French throne, French support for the Scots and French efforts to block the English wool trade in Belgium.

- **1337:** French king Philip VI tried to take over Guyenne. English king Edward III, whose mother was sister to three French kings, retaliated by claiming the French throne.

- **1340:** Edward won a great naval battle off Sluis, Belgium.

- **1346:** Edward III's archers – outnumbered 3 to 1 – routed the greatest French knights at Crécy with their great 2-m-long yew bows – and so hastened the end of knighthood.

- **1347:** Edward III took the French port of Calais.

- **1356:** Edward III's son, the Black Prince, won a great victory over the French at Poitiers.

- **1415:** the last great English victory was Henry V's at Agincourt. 6,000 English beat a French army of 30,000.

- **The English** won most battles, but the French won the war because they had three times the resources.

> ★ STAR FACT ★
> The tide turned for the French in 1429, when
> Joan of Arc led them to victory at Orléans.

The Hanseatic League

▶ Riches from the Hanseatic traders helped Hamburg build a great cathedral in the Middle Ages.

- **By the 1400s,** the feudal system of knights fighting part-time in exchange for land was outmoded. Kings now relied on full-time armies.

- **Kings turned** to newly rich merchants to pay for their armies, so merchants gained power. The Italians invented banks to give loans.

- **From the 1300s,** many serfs gained freedom and became prosperous 'yeoman' farmers. They needed merchants to sell their produce.

- **After the Crusades,** silks, spices and riches from the east were traded in the Mediterranean for cloth, hides and iron. In northern Europe, the wool trade thrived.

- **Trading towns** began to thrive across western Europe in the 1300s and 1400s – Antwerp, Flanders, Bruges, Bristol, Norwich, York, Florence, Venice, Milan and many others.

- **Trading towns** grew powerful. In England, many became boroughs with charters giving them some self-rule.

- **Merchants and traders** organized guilds (like trade unions) to defend their rights.

- **In 1241,** the German ports of Hamburg and Lübeck set up a *hanse* (guild) to protect merchants against pirates. The hanse grew to a very powerful Hanseatic League that monopolized trade around the Baltic Sea.

- **The Hanseatic League** set up special areas in cities across north Europe and controlled most trading routes. The League also put financial pressure on kings and lords to keep them at peace, and not to disrupt trade.

- **Hanseatic merchants** brought raw materials, spices and silks from eastern Europe and traded them for cloth, linen, silverware and woollen clothes from the west.

The Great Schism

- **In the Middle Ages,** kings and lords battled with the Church over who had the right to run people's lives.

- **The Church** was all-powerful but riddled with corruption. Men like John Wycliffe (1320-84) began to argue that it had too much power. He was supported by English kings.

- **In the 1100s,** scholars called 'scholastics' such as Roger Bacon tried to use reason to understand Christian ideas.

- **The French scholar** Peter Abelard argued that we should ask questions. 'By doubting, we come to inquiry, and by inquiry we come to truth.'

- **Churchmen** like Bernard of Clairvaux opposed scholastics: 'the faith of the righteous believes; it does not dispute.'

- **In 1302, Pope Boniface VIII** issued a decree called the *Unum sanctum* stating that everyone was subject to him.

- **French king** Philip IV said Boniface was trying to claim authority over the French king and French people.

- **In 1309,** Pope Clement V moved from Rome to Avignon in France. This became home to a series of French popes,

▶ *The Palace of the Popes in Avignon in southern France was built between 1314 and 1370. It was the home of the French popes for 100 years at the time of the Great Schism.*

until Pope Gregory XI went back to Rome in 1377.

- **When Gregory XI** died in 1378, there was a Great Schism (split) in the Church. Some claimed Italian Urban VI as pope. Others supported Robert from Switzerland. Urban stayed in Rome and Robert went back to Avignon. In 1409, some church leaders declared a third pope.

- **In 1417,** the Great Schism was ended when a council of all church leaders elected Martin V as pope in Rome. But the dispute had weakened the Church's authority fatally.

The Ottoman Wars

- **In 1281,** a new power began to emerge in Turkey from a tiny state called Sögüt, led by a ruler called Osman.

- **Over 200 years** a huge Muslim empire was built up, called the Ottoman Empire after Osman's descendants. It stretched from the Euphrates River on the borders of Persia to the Danube in Hungary.

- **In 1453,** Christian Constantinople fell to the Ottoman Turks and became their capital, Istanbul.

- **For centuries,** the Christian countries of Europe were threatened by Turkish expansion.

▶ *Lepanto was the last great battle between fleets of galleys – warships powered by huge banks of oarsmen.*

- **Ottoman power** peaked in the 1520s under Suleiman, known as *Qanuni* ('law-giver') by Turks and 'the Magnificent' by Europeans because of his splendid court.

- **Suleiman** took all Hungary and attacked Vienna in 1529.

- **In 1522,** Suleiman took the island of Rhodes from his sworn enemies, the Knights of St John, who moved to Malta and built the fort of Valetta.

- **In the 1520s,** the Turkish pirate Khir or *Barbarossa* (Spanish for Redbeard) took most of North Africa and became an Ottoman admiral. Algeria and the Barbary coast (North Africa) became a feared base for pirates for 300 years.

- **In 1565,** Suleiman attacked the Knights of St John in Valetta, but they survived.

- **When the Turks** attacked Cyprus in 1571, Venetian, Spanish and Papal fleets combined to crush them at the crucial battle of Lepanto in Greece. Turkish power declined after this.

The Wars of the Roses

- **The Wars of the Roses** were a series of civil wars fought in England in the 1400s as two branches of the Plantagenet family fought for the English throne.

- **On one side** was the house of York, with a white rose as its emblem. On the other was the house of Lancaster, with a red rose as its emblem.

- **The wars began** when Lancastrian king Henry VI became insane in 1453. With the country in chaos, Warwick the 'kingmaker' set up Richard, duke of York as Protector in Henry's place.

- **In 1455, Henry VI** seemed to recover and war broke out between Lancastrians and Yorkists.

- **Richard** was killed at the Battle of Wakefield in 1460, but Henry VI became insane again.

▶ The red rose and white rose were the emblems of the rival houses of Lancaster and York. When Henry VII wed Elizabeth of York, he combined the two to make the Tudor rose.

- **A crushing Yorkist victory** at Towton, near York, in 1461, put Richard's son on the throne as Edward IV.

- **Edward IV** made enemies of his brothers Clarence and Warwick, who invaded England from France in 1470 with Henry VI's queen Margaret of Anjou and drove Edward out.

- **Henry VI** was brought back for seven months before Edward's Yorkists defeated the Lancastrians at Barnet and Tewkesbury. Henry VI was murdered.

- **When Edward IV** died in 1483, his son Edward V was still a boy. When young Edward and his brother vanished – probably murdered in the Tower of London – their uncle Richard III seized the throne.

- **Richard III** made enemies among the Yorkists, who sided with Lancastrian Henry Tudor. Richard III was killed at Bosworth Field on 22 August 1485. Henry Tudor became Henry VII and married Elizabeth of York to end the wars.

Monasteries

- **Monasteries** played a key role in medieval life in Europe, reaching a peak in the 1200s.

- **The most famous monastery** was Cluny in France, but there were thousands of others in France and England.

- **Most monasteries** had a church called an abbey, some of which are among the greatest medieval buildings.

- **Monasteries** were the places where the poor went for welfare and they were also the only hospitals.

- **Monasteries** were places for scholars to study. They were the only libraries. Most great works of medieval art, literature and scholarship came from monasteries.

- **Monasteries** were great landowners with immense power and wealth. In England, monasteries owned a third of the land and a quarter of the country's wealth. They were also Europe's biggest single employers.

- **Many monasteries** oppressed the poor by taking over land and taking a heavy toll in tithes (church taxes).

- **Many monasteries** became notorious for the indulgence of their monks in fine food and high living.

- **New orders** of monks tried every now and then to go back to a simpler life, like the Cistercians from Citeaux in France and the Premonstratensians from Laon in France.

- **Cistercians** founded monasteries in barren places like Fountains in Yorkshire. But even they grew rich and lazy.

◀ Like most English monasteries, the great 12th-century Cistercian monastery at Tintern in Wales was destroyed by Henry VIII.

China

- **After almost a century** of chaos, the Song dynasty (family) of emperors came to power in China in AD960. The Songs ruled until the early 1200s, when the Mongol Khans invaded and their time is perhaps the golden age of Chinese civilization.

- **The Song rulers** renounced the warlike policies that had kept China in strife, and brought peace by paying tribute money to the barbarian peoples in the north. They had a huge army, but this was partly to give jobs to hundreds of thousands of poor Chinese.

- **The Song slowly got rid** of soldiers from government and replaced them with civil servants.

- **In earlier times,** only aristocrats tended to hold key posts in government, but under the Song, anyone could enter for the civil service exams. Competition to do well in the exams was intense, and the main yearly exams became major events in the calendar.

- **The civil service exams** stressed not practical skills but the study of literature and the classic works of the thinker Confucius. So the Song civil service was full of learned, cultured men, known in the west as mandarins. Ou Yang-hsiu was a typical mandarin – statesman, historian, poet, philosopher, wine and music connoisseur and brilliant player of the chess-like game *wei-ch'i*.

◀ Chinese porcelain and pottery is famous for its beauty and delicacy, and the perfection of the covering glaze. It reached a peak in the Ming era (1368-1644).

- **Under the Song,** the Chinese population soared, trade prospered and all kinds of advances were made in science and technology – from the invention of gunpowder and the sailors' compass to paper and printing. Technologically, China was about 500 years ahead of Europe.

- **The Song period** is also known for its exquisite landscape paintings and fine porcelain, which is why good porcelain is called 'China'.

- **In 1126,** barbarian invasions forced the Song to move their capital from Kaifeng in the north to Hangzhou (modern Shanghai) in the south.

- **By 1275,** Hangzhou was the world's largest city, with a population of a million. Its warm climate encouraged a lively, leisurely lifestyle. The city was full of luxury shops, bars, restaurants, tea-houses and clubs where girls sang. Often, people went out to stroll in the gardens by the West Lake or lazed over long meals on the lake's scores of floating restaurants, pushed along by poles like Venetian gondolas. Marco Polo later complained that the people here were 'anything but warriors; all their delight was in women, nothing but women.'

> ★ STAR FACT ★
> The Song inventions gunpowder and printing had a huge influence on Europe when they arrived there centuries later.

▶ When the Mongol Khans seized China from the Song, they made a new capital in the north at Beijing. At its centre lies a walled area containing the emperor's palaces. It is called the Forbidden City because only the emperor and his servants could enter it.

Joan of Arc

- **St Joan of Arc** (c.1412-31) was the peasant girl who led France from defeat in the Hundred Years' War and was burned at the stake for her beliefs.

- **Joan** was called Jeanne d'Arc in France. She called herself Jeanne la Pucelle (Joan the Maid).

- **Joan** was brought up in the village of Domrémy, near Nancy, northeastern France, as a shepherd girl.

- **By the age of 13,** Joan was having visions and believed that God had chosen her to help the French king Charles VII to beat the English.

- **Joan tried** to see the king but was laughed at until she was finally admitted to the king's court, in 1429.

- **To test Joan,** the king stood in disguise amongst his courtiers but Joan recognized him instantly – and also told him what he asked for in his secret prayers.

- **Joan was given** armour and an army to rescue the town of Orléans from the English and succeeded in just ten days.

▶ Shortly after her death, the pope pronounced Joan innocent of all crimes. She was later made a saint.

- **Joan then** led Charles VII through enemy territory to be crowned at Rheims cathedral.

- **In May 1430,** Joan was captured by the English and accused of witchcraft.

- **Joan insisted that** her visions came from God, so a tribunal of French clergy condemned her as a heretic. She was burned at the stake in Rouen on 30 May 1431.

Knights

▶ A knight's armour often weighed 25 kg so he had to be very fit in order to ride and fight in it.

- **Knights** were the elite fighting men of the Middle Ages, highly trained for combat both on horseback and on foot.

- **Knights always wore** armour. At first, the armour was simply shirts of mail, made from linked rings of iron. By the 1400s, most knights wore full suits of plate armour.

- **Knights rode into battle** on a horse called a *destrier*, or warhorse, and usually had an easy-going horse called a *palfry* just for when he was travelling, plus a packhorse called a *sumpter*.

- **Knights had a strict** code of honour called chivalry – from *chevalier*, the French for 'horseman'.

- **The ideal knight** was meant to be bold but good and gentle – fighting only to defend his lord, his lady and the Church. But in reality many were just brutal fighting men.

- **Training to be a knight** was a long and costly process, so most were from wealthy families.

- **A young boy** training to be a knight began at 7 as a page to a lord, then became a knight's squire (apprentice) at 14.

- **A squire's task** was to look after his master's armour, dress him for battle and serve his food.

- **A squire** who passed all the tests was dubbed a 'knight' at about 21 years old.

- **Knights took part** in mock battles called tournaments, often involving 'jousts', where two knights would charge at each other with lances.

The Renaissance

- **The Renaissance** was the great revolution in arts and ideas in Italy between the 1300s and the 1500s.

- **Renaissance** is French for 'rebirth', because it was partly about a revival of interest in the works of the classical world of Greece and Rome.

- **The Renaissance began** when many people started to doubt that the Church had all the answers.

- **Scholars** gradually developed the idea of 'humanism' – the idea that man is the focus of things, not God.

- **A spur** to the Renaissance was the fall of Constantinople in 1453. This sent Greek scholars fleeing to Italy, where they set up academies in cities like Florence and Padua.

- **Artists** in the Renaissance, inspired by classical examples, began to try and put people at the centre of their work – and to portray people and nature realistically rather than as religious symbols.

- **In the 1400s** brilliant artists like Donatello created startlingly realistic paintings and sculptures.

▶ The ancient Italian city of Padua is full of masterpieces of Renaissance building and art, including paintings by Giotto and sculptures by Donatello.

- **The three greatest artists** of the Renaissance were Michaelangelo, Raphael and Leonardo da Vinci.

- **The Renaissance** saw some of the world's greatest artistic and architectural masterpieces being created in Italian cities such as Florence and Padua.

- **During the late 1400s,** Renaissance ideas spread to northern Europe.

The Mogul Empire

- **The Moguls,** or Mughals, were a family who ruled most of northern India from 1526 to 1748.

- **The Moguls** were descended from the Mongol Ghengis Khan via Tamerlane – the great conqueror of the 1300s.

- **The first Mogul** emperor was Babur (1483-1530), who invaded India on swift horses that completely outran the Indians' slower elephants.

- **Babur** was a brave and brilliant leader, as well as a famous poet and diarist.

- **Babur** created gardens wherever he went and held garden parties there when they were finished.

▶ Jahangir's father Akbar (right) called his son plain Salim. He called himself Jahangir ('world beater').

- **After Babur** came a string of remarkable emperors: Humayun, Akbar, Jahangir, Shah Jahan and Aurangzeb.

- **Akbar** (1556-1605) was the greatest of the Mogul emperors – conquering most of India and setting up a highly efficient system of government.

- **Jahangir** (1569-1627) was a great patron of the arts – but suffered from an addiction to drugs and alcohol. He was also attacked for being under the thumb of his Persian wife, Nur Jahan.

- **The Mogul Empire** reached its peak under Shah Jahan (1592-1666), when many magnificent, luxurious buildings were built – most notably the Taj Mahal.

- **Aurangzeb** (1618-1707) was the last great Mogul ruler. He inspired rebellion by raising taxes and insisting on a strict Muslim code.

Voyages of exploration

- **In the late 1300s,** the Mongol Empire in Asia collapsed and Ottoman Turks grew powerful in the Near East. The roads to China and the east that brought silks and spices to Europe were cut off.

- **Italian merchant cities** like Genoa and Venice needed another route. So bold sailors set out from Portugal and Spain to find a way to the east by sea.

- **At first,** they tried to go round Africa, and voyages ventured down Africa's unknown west coast.

- **Many early voyages** were encouraged by Portugal's Prince Henry (1394-1460), called Henry the Navigator, who set up a school in navigation skills at Sagres.

- **In 1488,** Bartholomeu Dias sailed right round Africa's southern tip and into the Indian Ocean.

- **In 1497,** Vasco da Gama sailed round Africa to Calicut in India, and returned laden with spices and jewels.

- **Perhaps the greatest** voyage by a European was in 1492 when Genoese sailor Christopher Columbus set out across the open Atlantic. He hoped to reach China by travelling westwards around the world. Instead, he found the whole 'New World', North and South America.

- **Columbus** only landed on Caribbean islands at first. Even when he reached South America on his last voyage, he thought he was in Asia. The first to realize it was an unknown continent was the Florentine explorer Amerigo Vespucci who landed there in 1499. A map made in 1507 named North and South America after him.

- **In 1519-22,** Ferdinand Magellan's ship *Victoria* sailed across the Atlantic, round the southern tip of South America, across the Pacific and back round Africa to Spain. Although this Portuguese explorer was killed in the Philippines, his crew and ship went on to complete the first round-the-world voyage.

A lookout in the crow's nest often saw new land first

A triangular lateen sail on the mizzen (rear) mast helped the ship sail into the wind and manoeuvre along coasts

A small poop (raised deck) held the captain's cabin

Big square sails on the fore and main masts filled like parachutes for high-speed sailing

> ★ **STAR FACT** ★
> Venetian John Cabot set out from Bristol, England in 1497 – and 'discovered' North America when he landed in Labrador.

◀ Nearly all the great European explorers of the 1400s and 1500s – Dias, Columbus, da Gama, Vespucci, Cabot and others – sailed in a remarkable little ship called a caravel. Caravels were a revolutionary mix of European and Arab shipbuilding methods. They were rarely more than 20-30 m long and weighed under 150 tonnes. But they could cope with the roughest seas. More importantly, they could head almost into the wind, so they could sail in most directions. They were also very fast – vital for exploration when crossing vast oceans.

A raised section at the bow called the forecastle gave extra storm protection and extra accommodation

The caravel's strong deck was a platform for guns and made it very storm-proof

The caravel had a deep, narrow hull and a strong, straight keel for speed and stability

The Medicis

- **The Medici family** of Florence in Italy were one of the richest and most powerful families in Europe between 1400 and 1700.
- **The Medicis' fortunes** began with the bank founded by Cosimo de' Medici in 1397. The bank was a success and the Medicis became staggeringly rich.
- **Cosimo's son,** Cosimo, built up the bank and there were soon branches in every major city in Europe.
- **By 1434,** Cosimo was so rich and powerful that he became ruler of Florence. Except for brief periods, the Medicis then ruled Florence for 300 years.
- **The Medicis** were famed for paying huge sums of money to commission works of art.
- **The artist** Michelangelo worked for the Medicis from 1515 to 1534 and created the fabulous Medici chapel for them.
- **The most famous Medici** was Lorenzo (1449-92), known as the Magnificent. Under him, Florence became Europe's most splendid city, full of great works of art.

▶ *Lorenzo de' Medici was a tough ruler who put down opposition brutally. But he was also a scholar and a fine poet.*

- **Lorenzo** may have been Magnificent, but he managed to bankrupt the Medici bank.
- **Three Medicis** became pope – Leo X (1513-21), Clement VII (1523-34) and then Leo XI (1605).
- **Two Medicis** became queens of France. One of these was Catherine de' Medici (1519-89), queen of Henry II .

The Incas

▶ *The Inca ruler was called the Sapa Inca, and he was thought of as the son of the sun, a living god. His main wife or ccoya was his sister.*

- **The Incas** were South American people who created a remarkable empire in the Americas in the 1400s.
- **The Incas** began as a tribe in highland Peru, but in 1438 Pachacuti Inca Yupanqui became their Sapa Inca (king) and they built a huge empire in an amazingly short time.
- **Pachacuti** and his son built a huge empire in just 50 years stretching 4,000 km through what is now Peru and Chile.
- **Inca soldiers** were highly disciplined and deadly with slings, bronze axes and spears.
- **Inca engineers** swiftly built 30,000 km of paved roads across the empire, spanning deep ravines with dizzying suspension bridges.
- **The Incas** kept in close touch with local officials by relays of runners 2.5 km apart. A message could travel 250 km in under a day.
- **Inca builders** cut and fitted huge stones with astonishing precision to create massive buildings.
- **The royal palace** had a garden full of life-like corn stalks, animals and birds made of solid gold.
- **The Incas** worshipped the sun.

> ★ STAR FACT ★
> The Inca capital was called Cuzco, which means 'navel' because it was the centre of their world.

Christopher Columbus

- **Christopher Columbus** (1451-1596) was the Genoese sailor who crossed the Atlantic and showed North and South America to Europe.

- **Columbus** was not the first European to cross the Atlantic. The Vikings, for instance, settled in Newfoundland in AD1004. But it is Columbus's discovery that lasted.

- **Other sailors** were trying to find their way to China and the east by sailing south round Africa. Columbus, realizing the Earth is round, wanted to strike out west across the open Atlantic ocean and reach China that way.

- **After years spent trying** to get backing Columbus finally got support from Queen Isabella of Spain.

- **Columbus set sail** on 3 August 1492 in three caravels – the *Santa Maria*, the *Niña* and the *Pinta*.

◀ Columbus's first and last voyages.

NORTH AMERICA
EUROPE
AFRICA
SOUTH AMERICA

1st voyage 1492-93
4th voyage 1502-04

- **They sailed west** into the unknown for three weeks, by which time the sailors were ready to mutiny with fear.

- **On 12 October,** a look-out spotted the Bahamas. Columbus thought he was in the Indies (hence the 'West Indies'). He called the natives Indians.

- **Columbus** left 40 men on a large island that he called Hispaniola and went back to Spain a hero.

- **In 1493 and 1498,** he set off on two more trips with large fleets, as Viceroy of the Indies. He set up a colony on Hispaniola, but it was a disaster. Spaniards complained of his harsh rule and millions of Indians died from cruelty and disease. Columbus went back to Spain in chains.

- **Columbus** was pardoned, and began a fourth voyage in 1502. He died off Panama, still thinking it was India.

The Reformation

◀ Martin Luther was the friar whose radical views sparked off the great Reformation, which divided Christians in Europe into Catholics and Protestants.

- **In the early 1500s,** many people were starting to question the Catholic Church. They were angered by the excessive power of church leaders and the life of pleasure that many monks seemed to lead.

- **Many critics were angered** by the huge amounts of money the Church made by selling 'indulgences' – a pardon for sin bought with cash.

- **Martin Luther** (1483-1546) was a poor miner's son from Saxony in Germany. As a friar at Wittenberg university, he earned a reputation for his great biblical knowledge.

- **Luther** attacked the sale of indulgences by Pope Leo X, who was selling them by the score to raise money to build St Peter's church in Rome.

- **In 1517,** Luther nailed a list of 95 grievances on the door of Wittenberg Castle's chapel, hoping to start a debate.

- **The pope** issued a bull (demand) that Luther go back on his views or face expulsion from the Church. Luther burned the bull – and the Church expelled him in 1521.

- **The development of printing in Europe in the 1400s** meant that pamphlets explaining Luther's views could be read by thousands, and support grew rapidly.

- **Luther set up** his own church, whose members soon came to be called Protestants – because of their protests.

- **Other more extreme rebels** joined the cause, such as John Calvin (1509-64) and Huldreich Zwingli, and the movement gathered pace across northwest Europe.

- **Soon the Protestant** movement was so strong and widespread that the split with the Catholic Church seemed permanent. This is called the Reformation.

The conquistadors

- **The conquistadors** ('conquerors') were Spaniards who landed in the 'New World' shortly after Columbus. They came to conquer the peoples there.
- **The most famous** conquistadors were Hernán Cortés (1485-1547) and Francisco Pizarro (c.1478-1541).
- **Cortés landed** in Mexico with just 500 men in 1519. The Indian girl Malintzin became his interpreter and lover.
- **Joining** with Indians rebelling against the Aztecs, he marched to Tenochtitlán, the Aztec capital.
- **Perhaps thinking** that Cortés was the god Quetzalcoatl, the Aztec leader Moctezuma let Cortés take him prisoner and become ruler in his place.
- **When Cortés** left Tenochtitlán six months later, the Aztecs rebelled. Cortés returned and destroyed the city.

> ★ STAR FACT ★
> When Spaniards got off their horses, the Incas thought they were beasts splitting in two.

▲ *A Spaniard's fanciful view of Cortés in Tenochtitlán.*

- **Pizarro** set off to find the Incas in 1524.
- **Pizarro** reached Peru when the Incas were hardly over a civil war between the Inca Atahualpa and his brother.
- **The Incas,** terrified of Pizarro's horses and guns, were easily slaughtered. Pizarro took Cuzco in 1533.

Shoguns and samurai

- **In the 12th century,** the civilized Japanese Fujiwara rulers were replaced by powerful warrior clans from country areas – notably the Taira and Minamoto.
- **In 1185,** the Minamoto Yoritomo crushed the Taira clan and made himself ruler of Japan as *sei-i-dai-shogun* which means 'barbarian conquering great general'.
- **Warrior shoguns** ruled Japan until the mid-1800s.
- **Japan** became dominated by *samurai*. The samurai warriors lived to fight and trained in fighting skills to a fanatical degree.
- **A samurai's prized possession** was his massive two-handed sword, which was sharpened and honed to such an extent that a skilled samurai could slice a man in half with a single stroke.

- **Samurai** means 'one who serves'.
- **The warrior culture** drove many to seek refuge in nature and men started to live for long periods in remote huts.
- **A kind of Buddhism** called Zen appealed to many Japanese. It showed how meditation could make then see beyond the material world.
- **In the 1300s** Samurai began to take a more Zen approach to their skills.
- **In the 1300s** these Zen Buddhists began to develop their own forms of elegant entertainment, like flower-arranging and tea-drinking.

◄ *Samurai warriors dominated Japan for centuries.*

Henry VIII

- **Henry VIII** (1491-1547) was the Tudor king of England who separated the Church in England from Rome, and who married six wives, beheading two of them.

- **Henry's wives:** Catherine of Aragon (1509-33, divorced); Anne Boleyn (1533-36, beheaded); Jane Seymour (1536-38, died); Anne of Cleves (1540, annulled); Catherine Howard (1540-42, beheaded); and Catherine Parr (1543-47).

- **When Henry VIII** became king at 18, in 1509, he was handsome and athletic, spoke several languages, played the lute well and was keen on new 'humanist' ideas. As he grew old, he became grossly fat, riddled with sickness and inclined to terrible outbreaks of anger.

- **Henry was served** by clever ministers like Wolsey and Cromwell. Many were executed when things went wrong.

- **Catherine of Aragon** bore Henry a daughter, Mary, but not the needed son. The pope refused a divorce, so Henry broke with Rome to become head of the English Church.

- **Split from Rome,** the Church of England moved towards Protestantism and the monasteries were destroyed.

- **Anne Boleyn** gave Henry a daughter, Elizabeth, but not the son he wanted, and her strong views made her enemies. She was beheaded on a charge of treason.

- **Jane Seymour** gave Henry a son, Edward, but died in childbirth in 1538.

- **Henry** found Anne of Cleves so ugly, he cancelled the marriage after five months.

- **Young Catherine Howard** was beheaded when she was found to have a lover. Only Henry's last wife, twice-widowed Catherine Parr, survived him when he died in 1547.

▶ *We have an astonishingly clear picture of what Henry and his court looked like from the brilliant portraits of Hans Holbein. This picture is based on Holbein's striking painting of Henry from 1537.*

Catholics v Protestants

◀ *Thomas More (1478-1535) was executed in when he refused to acknowledge Henry VIII as head of the English Church.*

- **In the 1500s** the Roman Catholic church was determined to fight against the Protestant Reformation and other threats. Their fight is called the Counter-Reformation.

- **In 1534,** St Ignatius Loyola founded the Society of Jesus (Jesuits) to lead the Counter-Reformation.

- **Investigative bodies** called Inquisitions were set up to seek out and punish heretics – anyone who held views that did not agree with the Catholic Church's.

- **From 1483,** the Spanish Inquisition became a byword for terror, swooping on suspected heretics – Protestants and Jews alike – torturing them and burning them at the stake.

- **The battle between** Catholics and Protestants created many victims and many martyrs in the late 1500s.

- **In the St Bartholomew's Day massacre** in 1571, up to 70,000 French Protestants, called Huguenots, were killed on the orders of the Catholic queen Catherine de' Medici.

- **English Protestants** like Tyndale were burned in Catholic Queen Mary's reign, earning her the name 'Bloody Mary'.

- **English Catholics** such as Edmund Campion (1540-1581) were beheaded in Protestant Queen Elizabeth I's reign.

- **In Germany,** a terrible Thirty Years' War was started in 1618 as Catholic-Protestant rivalries flared up.

★ STAR FACT ★
Catholic houses in England in the late 1500s had hiding places for priests called 'priest holes'.

The Spanish Empire

- **Within half a century** of Columbus's arrival in America in 1492, Spanish conquistadors had conquered all of what is now often called Latin America – from California to Argentina. This huge empire – the biggest yet seen in the world – became an immense source of wealth.

- **By the Treaty of Tordesillas (1494)** Portugal agreed to allow Spain to take any territory more than 370 leagues (about 2,000 km) west of the Cape Verde islands – all of Latin America but Brazil.

- **Thousands of Spaniards** came to colonize Latin America in the 1500s, creating Spanish-style cities such as Cartagena in Colombia and Guayaqil in Ecuador.

- **The Spanish rulers** tried to deal with local people with the *encomienda*. Native Americans were assigned to Spaniards who were supposed to look after them in return for taxes and labour. In practice, many Spaniards were cruel to these people, and Spaniards now talk of how cruelly they abused the Native Americans. In 100 years, the number of Native Americans dropped from 50 million to 4 million, through cruelty, poverty and diseases brought by Spaniards.

- **Many Spanish Dominican friars** condemned the encomienda – especially Bartolomé de Las Casas – and fought unsuccessfully for better conditions for Native Americans.

◀ Most American gold and silver was melted into bars and stamped with the king's seal to go back to Spain. Some was minted into coins like these, such as the famous gold 'doubloon' (eight escudos) and silver 'pieces of eight' (eight reale).

- **Indians used** to mine silver, gold and gems in huge quantities in South America. The Muzo and Chivor mines in Colombia were famous for their emeralds.

- **Every year,** in the calm months between March and October, ships laden with treasure left the Americas bound for Spain.

- **Besides American** treasure, Spanish ships carried spices from the East Indies and silks from China. These were shipped across the Pacific from the Philippines to Mexico, then carried overland to be shipped from the Caribbean to Europe.

- **By the 1540s,** the Spanish ships were suffering pirate attacks, so the ships crossed the Atlantic every year in two great *flotas* (fleets) protected by an armada of galleons (warships).

> ★ STAR FACT ★
> The Spanish brought new foods such as tomatoes, potatoes and chocolate back to Europe from their American empire.

Three masts with square sails – or, as here, with a triangular lateen on the mizzen (rear) mast

Banks of 20 or so cannon for 'broadsides' – firing together down one side

▶ Late August every year, the two Spanish treasure fleets of 50 or so ships would leave together from Havana in Cuba guarded by the galleons of the Armada de la Guardia. Galleons (right) were the biggest, most powerful warships of the day, 35 m long and weighing around 500 tonnes.

Hull and decking of winter-cut oak, cedar or cypress hardwood

Elizabeth I

- **Elizabeth I** (1533-1603) was one of England's greatest rulers. The time of her reign is called the Elizabethan Age or England's Golden Age. Under her strong and intelligent rule, England became an enterprising, artistically rich and peaceful nation.
- **Elizabeth** was daughter of Henry VIII and his wife Anne Boleyn, who was beheaded when Elizabeth was three.
- **Elizabeth** was a brilliant scholar, fluent in many languages by the time she was 12.
- **When Henry VIII died,** Elizabeth's nine-year-old half-brother became King Edward VI, but he died in 1553. He was succeeded by her older sister 'Bloody' Mary.
- **Mary was** staunchly Catholic. For a while Elizabeth was locked up, suspected of involvement in a Protestant plot.
- **Elizabeth became queen** in 1558, when Mary died.

◀ With the aid of poets like Spenser and painters like Nicholas Hilliard, Elizabeth created a dazzling image for herself. She was linked to Diana the virgin huntress god and Gloriana, Spenser's fairy queen.

- **At once** Elizabeth strengthened the Protestant Church of England by the Act of Supremacy in 1559.
- **Elizabeth was expected** to marry, and she encouraged foreign suitors when it helped diplomacy. But she remained single, earning her the nickname 'The Virgin Queen'.
- **Elizabeth** sent troops to help Protestants in Holland against their Spanish rulers, and secretly urged Francis Drake to raid Spanish treasure ships. In 1588 Spain sent an Armada to invade England. Elizabeth proved an inspiring leader and the Armada was repulsed.
- **Elizabeth's reign** is famed for the poetry and plays of men like Spenser, Marlowe and Shakespeare.

Colonization of America

- **In the 1580s,** English people tried unsuccessfully to set up colonies in North America.
- **The first successful English colony** was set up at Jamestown, Virginia on 24 May 1607, with 104 colonists.
- **Many of the Jamestown colony** died in 'the starving time' of winter 1609.
- **In 1610,** fighting broke out with the local Indians as the desperate colonists took the Indians' food supply.

★ STAR FACT ★
Pocahontas died of smallpox while in London trying to raise money for the colonists.

- **Colonist leader** John Smith was captured by the Indians, but the chief's daughter Pocahontas saved his life.
- **In 1612,** colonist John Rolfe introduced tobacco from the West Indies. It became the basis of Virginia's economy.
- **Pocahontas** was held hostage by the colonists in 1613. While captive she met, fell in love with and wed John Rolfe.
- **In 1621,** 102 'Pilgrims' arrived from Plymouth, England in the *Mayflower* and set up a new colony near Cape Cod. They survived thanks to help from Wampanoag Indians.
- **In November 1621** the Pilgrims invited the Wampanoags to celebrate their first harvest. This first Thanksgiving Day is now celebrated every year in the USA.

◀ Some of the simple houses lived in by the Jamestown colonists have been recreated in this museum in Virginia.

Dutch independence

- **In 1500** there were 17 provinces making up what is now Belgium, the Netherlands and Luxembourg. The most important was Holland.

- **The provinces came** under Spanish rule in 1516, when their ruler Charles became the king of Spain.

▶ *In the 1400-1600s, Dutch artists like Steen, Vermeer and Rembrandt created vibrant, technically brilliant paintings, often of everyday scenes. This is by Van Eyck, who was said to have invented oil painting in the 1430s.*

- **In the 1500s,** Holland's capital Amsterdam became the leading commercial centre of Europe. With the growth of trade, Protestant ideas started taking hold.

- **Charles's son** Philip II and his deputy the duke of Alba tried to crush the Protestants by executing their leaders.

- **As Alba** became more ruthless, opposition spread.

- **In 1566,** William, prince of Orange, led the Dutch in revolt. Although the Dutch controlled the sea, they gradually gave way before the Spanish army.

- **In 1574,** the Dutch opened dikes holding back the sea to sail over the flood to Leiden and rescue the besieged.

- **Protestants** retreated to the northern provinces, and in 1581 declared themselves the independent Dutch Republic. The fighting ceased.

- **The 1600s** proved a Golden Age for the Dutch Republic.

- **The Dutch** merchant fleet became the biggest in Europe. Dutch banks and businesses thrived and Dutch scientists like Leeuwenhoek and Huygens made great discoveries.

Toyotomi Hideyoshi

- **Toyotomi Hideyoshi** (1536-81) was the great Japanese shogun who unified Japan.

- **Hideyoshi** was the son of poor, hard-working peasants.

- **As a boy,** Hideyoshi believed that if he became a shogun, he'd make sure peasants wouldn't have to work so hard.

- **As a man,** Hideyoshi became a soldier for shogun Oda Nobunaga, who was trying to unify Japan through force.

- **One day,** legend says, Hideyoshi warmed Nobunaga's shoes for a winter walk. Nobunaga made him a general.

- **Hideyoshi** proved himself a brilliant general, and when Nobunaga was murdered, Hideyoshi carried on his work in unifying Japan – but by good rule as well as by arms.

- **By 1591,** Hideyoshi had unified Japan, but he kept warriors and peasants firmly separated as classes.

- **To establish** a mystique for his court, Hideyoshi had the Zen master Sen Rikyu perfect the tea ceremony.

- **Later, Hideyoshi** became paranoid. Suspecting his chief adviser Hidetsugu of plotting, he had Hidetsugu's family killed – including the beautiful Princess Komahime.

- **Komahime's father** Yoshiaki sided decisively with Hideyoshi's enemy, the hero Tokugawa Ieyasu, in the great battle that led to Hideyoshi's downfall.

▼ *Great tea masters claim descent from Sen Rikyu, who Hideyoshi forced to commit suicide when he suspected a slight to him.*

Russia

- **In 1237,** savage Tatar hordes, the descendants of Genghis Khan, swept into Russia, burning cities and slaughtering huge numbers of people. The Tatars stayed there for 200 years, cutting Russia off from the Renaissance that was changing western Europe.

- **Some Russians** thrived under the Tatars and a trading post called Moscow grew into a powerful city at the centre of a province called Muscovy. In 1318, Prince Yuri of Moscow married the Tatar Khan's sister, and the Tatars helped Moscow ruthlessly suppress rivals. A later prince called Ivan began collecting taxes for the Tatars.

- **Moscow** grew stronger as the Tatars grew weaker. In 1453, Ivan III ('the Great'), Grand Prince of Muscovy, was strong enough to drive out the Tatars altogether.

- **Russians were Christians** of the Eastern Church ruled from Constantinople. Constantinople had become the second focus of Christianity when Rome fell to barbarians in the AD400s. When Constantinople fell to the Turks in 1453, Ivan III called for Moscow to be the Third Rome. He wed a Byzantine princess, and his grandson Ivan IV took the title czar after the Roman caesars.

- **Ivan's** ambitions left him in need of money and food, so he forced thousands of peasants into serfdom – at a time when peasants in western Europe were gaining their freedom. Those who would not submit to this yoke fled to the southern steppes, where they became known as Cossacks.

▶ Ivan the Terrible was a clever man, notorious for his biting sarcasm as well as his rages. But no one really knows just how 'terrible' he was.

- **Ivan IV** (1544-84), the first czar, drove the Tatars out of Russia altogether, conquering Kazan, Astrakhan and much of Siberia – creating the first Russian Empire.

- **Ivan IV** was called 'the Terrible' for his brutality. He formed the *Oprichniki* – a police force to control people – and had hundreds of *boyars* (aristocrats) murdered. He even beat his son Ivan to death in a fit of rage.

- **Ivan IV was** an effective ruler, who encouraged scholars and brought Moscow its first printing presses.

- **Ivan IV's second son** Fyodor was a simpleton, and his wife's brother Boris Godunov seized the throne in 1598.

- **When Godunov died** in 1606, Moscow fell into a period of chaos called the 'Time of Troubles'. A monk called Gregory Otrepiev claimed to be Dmitry, another of Ivan IV's sons who was thought to have died. He invaded Moscow with a Polish army and rebellious Cossacks, and Russia was torn apart by civil war.

▲▶ Under Ivan the Great and his grandson Ivan the Terrible, Moscow grew to become the centre of a vast Russian empire, which survived up until the time of the Russian Revolution in 1917. Ivan rebuilt Moscow's citadel, or Kremlin, as a vast walled complex of palaces and churches (above). It has remained the centre of Russian government ever since.

Mary Queen of Scots

- **Mary Queen of Scots** (1542-87) was the Catholic queen of Scotland held captive in England by Elizabeth I for 19 years, then beheaded.
- **Mary became queen** when she was a baby but was brought up at the French court, where she enjoyed hunting and learned six languages.
- **Mary married** the French king Henry II's son Francis at 15 and was briefly queen of France, but Francis died in 1560.
- **In 1561,** Mary returned to Scotland to rule there. By this time, Scotland had become Protestant, while Mary was a Catholic.
- **In 1565,** Mary fell in love with her cousin Henry Stuart, Earl of Darnley. She married him and they had a child, but Darnley was only interested in power.
- **Led by Darnley,** Protestant nobles stabbed Mary's Catholic secretary David Rizzio to death before her.
- **The Earl of Bothwell** was in love with Mary and murdered Darnley. They married three months later.

◄ Mary was a romantic figure – young, beautiful and passionate and ever inclined to follow her heart, not her head. No wonder so many young Catholic men dreamed of rescuing her from captivity.

The Scots were so outraged by the marriage that Mary had to flee to England.

- **Mary** was next in line to the English throne after Elizabeth. Many Catholics felt she was first in line, since they did not recognize Henry VIII's marriage to Anne Boleyn.
- **Mary** posed a danger to Elizabeth, so she was kept in captivity in English houses, where she became the focus for plots against Elizabeth.
- **Elizabeth's spy-master** Walsingham trapped Mary into going along with a plot by Babington. Mary was found guilty of treason and beheaded at Fotheringay in 1587.

Native Americans

> ★ STAR FACT ★
> Woodland tribes lived in wigwams, domes of sticks covered in hide and moss.

- **When the first European colonists** arrived in North America, there were one and a half million Native Americans living in North America.
- **There were hundreds** of tribes in North America, each with its own language.
- **There were six** kinds of tribal area: the Southwest, Great Plains, Far West Plateau, Northwest, Eastern Woodland and Northern.
- **Southwest** Native Americans like the Pueblo Indians lived by growing corn, beans and squash.
- **Plains** tribes like the Blackfoot, Comanche and Cheyenne hunted buffalo on foot.
- **With Woodland tribes** like the Delaware, the men hunted deer and fished while the women grew crops.

- **Plateau and Northwest** Native Americans like the Nez Percé and the Kwakiutl lived by fishing and gathering berries. They are famous for their baskets.
- **Northern** tribes like the Cree lived mainly by hunting caribou.
- **Until Europeans** arrived, Native Americans got around mainly on foot or by canoe. The Europeans introduced horses in the 1700s – and Indians quickly became skilled riders.

▶ North American Indians wore clothes of buckskin (tanned deer hide). They adorned the costume with eagle feathers, which had special significance.

The Manchus

▲ *Under the Qing, China remained as it had been for 3,000 years, while much of the world was changing dramatically.*

- **In the 1600s,** the Ming emperors of China were unpopular after three centuries in power. Rebellions became all too common.

- **In 1644,** the last Ming emperor hanged himself as the bandit Li Zicheng and his men overran Beijing.

- **Guarding the Great Wall** were Manchu troops, from Manchuria in the north. A desperate Ming general invited them to help get rid of Li Zicheng.

- **The Manchus** marched into Beijing and proclaimed their own child-emperor as the 'Son of Heaven' and set up the Qing dynasty of emperors.

- **Resistance** to the Manchu emperors went on in the south for 30 years, but was eventually suppressed.

- **At first, the Qing** forced Chinese men to put their hair in pigtails to show they were inferior to Manchus.

- **Manchus** and Chinese were also made to live separately and were not allowed to marry each other.

- **In time,** the Qing adopted Chinese ways, and even Manchu civil servants had to learn the classic works of Confucius, just like the Chinese.

- **Under the Qing,** China reached its greatest extent.

- **In the 1800s,** Qing power was weakened by rebellions, Muslim uprisings and growing European influence.

Roundheads and Cavaliers

- **The English Civil War** (1642-49) was the struggle between 'Cavalier' supporters of King Charles I and 'Roundheads', who supported Parliament.

- **A key issue** was how much power the king should have. Charles wanted to be free to set taxes and his own brand of religion. Parliament demanded a say.

- **On the royalist side** were Anglicans, who wanted the English Church more Catholic; on the other were Puritans.

- **Puritans** were extreme Protestants. They believed that churches (and people) should be stripped of the wasteful luxury they saw in the Catholic Church and the aristocrats at the court of Charles's French, Catholic wife.

▶ *Many Cavaliers had long hair and wore colourful French clothes. Some, like Lovelace, were poets.*

- **'Cavalier'** is from the French *chevalier* (horseman). It was meant as a term of abuse. Many Cavaliers were rich landowners.

- **Puritans** thought long hair indulgent, and the Roundheads got their name from their short-cropped hair. Many Roundheads were rich merchants and townspeople.

- **Many revolutionary groups** emerged among poorer people, such as the 'Diggers' and 'Levellers'.

- **The war** turned against the royalists when the parliamentarians formed the disciplined New Model Army.

- **Charles I** was beheaded in 1649.

- **Oliver Cromwell** (1599-1658) became Roundhead leader and signed Charles I's death warrant. In 1653, he made himself Lord Protector – England's dictator.

The Sun King

- **Louis XIV** (1638-1715) was king of France for 72 years, a longer reign than any other European king in history.
- **Louis** became king in 1643, when he was five, and the first minister Cardinal Mazarin effectively ruled France.
- **In 1648,** heavy taxes and other grievances inspired a rebellion – the Fronde – against the hated Mazarin.
- **During the Fronde,** Louis was forced into hiding, and vowed never to let the same happen again.

> ★ STAR FACT ★
> Louis's magnificent new palace at Versailles took 36,000 workers 47 years to build.

- **Louis** said *L'état c'est moi* ('I am the State') and believed it was his God-given right to command his people totally.
- **When Mazarin died,** in 1661, Louis decided to run the country himself, and devoted huge energy to administering every detail of the nation's business.
- **Louis** made France the most efficiently run country in Europe. It hummed with new industries, road and canals.
- **Louis** used the finest artists to turn the French court into a glittering spectacle to distract nobles from rebellion. His palace was filled with banquets, plays and art.
- **Louis** got the nickname 'The Sun King' from his favourite dance role, that of Apollo the Sun God. He adopted the Sun as his emblem.

◀ *Part of Louis's grand palace at Versailles, just outside Paris.*

Gustavus Adolphus

- **Gustavus Adolphus** (1594-1632) was Sweden's greatest king and military leader.
- **Gustavus** was a brilliant speaker and inspiring general who always led his men into battle from the front.
- **Gustavus** had a perfect ally in his chancellor Axel Oxenstierna (said 'erks'n'sherna'). Gustavus ran the foreign wars while Oxenstierna ran Sweden.
- **When Gustavus came** to the throne at the age of 17, Sweden was involved in three wars: with Denmark (1611-13), Russia (1611-17) and Poland.
- **Gustavus** quickly made peace with Denmark and Russia.
- **In skirmishes** with the Poles, Gustavus began to develop the first modern army – a large, highly mobile force combining foot soldiers and horsemen.
- **Gustavus** was a devout Protestant. When he saw the Protestants of Germany facing defeat in the Thirty Years' War against the Catholic Austrian emperor Ferdinand II, he decided to intervene.

- **In July 1630,** Gustavus's armies landed in Germany.
- **In 1631,** Gustavus won a great victory over Ferdinand's army at Breitenfeld near Leipzig.
- **On 6 Nov 1632,** the Swedes scored a crucial victory over Bohemian general Wallenstein, but Gustavus himself was killed leading a charge.

▶ *Gustavus's great flagship, the Vasa, sank on its maiden voyage in 1628, but it has been recovered almost intact and can now be seen in Stockholm.*

Pirates

- **Barbary corsairs** were pirates from North Africa who raided ships in the Mediterranean between 1520 and 1830. Many corsairs were Muslims and regarded Christian merchant ships as fair game.

- **The most famous** corsairs were the Barbarossa brothers and Occhiali.

- **Sea dogs** were pirates like Sir Francis Drake, secretly encouraged by Queen Elizabeth I to raid the ships of her Spanish enemies in the Caribbean.

- **'Letters of marque'** from the monarch gave English raiders official blessing, so they were called privateers.

- **When King James I** withdrew letters of marque in 1603, privateers were replaced by lawless 'buccaneers' like Henry Morgan, who terrorized the Caribbean from bases on Jamaica like Port Royal.

◀ *The famous 'Jolly Roger' flag, flown from pirate ships.*

- **Buccaneer** comes from French *boucan* (barbeque) as many were poor hunters who grilled the meat of cows and pigs that they scavenged.

- **Piracy** reached its height between 1690 and 1790, preying on traders plying between Europe and its new colonies around the world.

- **In the Indian Ocean** were pirates like William Kidd from Madagascar. In the Bahamas, there were 'Calico Jack' Rackham and female pirates Anne Bonny and Mary Read.

- **The most notorious** pirate of this time was 'Blackbeard' (Edward Teach), who leaped into action with lighted firecrackers tied to his big black beard.

- **Piracy** diminished after 1720, when the British navy clamped down worldwide.

The Restoration

- **For 11 years** after the execution of Charles I in 1649, England was without a king. It was ruled instead by the Commonwealth, run by the Puritans.

- **At first,** the Commonwealth consisted of Parliament and its Council of State, but its failure to make progress spurred general Oliver Cromwell to make himself Lord Protector and rule through army officers.

- **Cromwell's Protectorate** proved unpopular. When he died in 1658, the army removed his son Richard Cromwell as successor and called for Charles I's exiled son Charles II to be recalled as king.

◀ *The sedan chair was a popular way for the rich to get about in the years after the Restoration.*

> ★ **STAR FACT** ★
> When London burned down, in 1666, Charles II personally organized the fire-fighting.

- **The Restoration** of Charles II as king was in May 1660.

- **Charles II** proved on the whole a skilful ruler, tactfully easing tensions between rival religious groups.

- **Charles II** was known as the Merry Monarch, because his love of partying, theatre, horse-racing and women was such a relief after years of grim Puritan rule.

- **Charles II** had many mistresses. The most famous was Nell Gwyn, an orange-seller who worked in the theatres.

- **The Restoration** saw the Puritan ban on Christmas and the theatre lifted. Plays like Congreve's *Way of the World* made Restoration theatre lively and outrageous.

- **Charles II** took a keen interest in science, encouraging great scientists like Isaac Newton, Edmund Halley and Robert Hooke to form the Royal Society.

Slavery

- **Slaves** were used a great deal in the ancient world, as warring people put their captives to work. The pyramids of Egypt were probably built mostly by slaves. One in three people in Ancient Athens was likely to have been a slave.

- **Slavery** diminished in Europe when Rome collapsed, although in the Middle Ages Russian and African slaves were used on sugar plantations in the Mediterranean.

- **Slavery** grew hugely when Europeans established colonies in the Americas from the 1500s on.

- **At first,** the settlers used Native Americans as slaves, but as numbers dwindled, they took slaves from Africa to work on new sugar plantations. British and French sugar planters in the West Indies used African slaves too.

- **From 1500-1800,** Europeans shipped 10-12 million black slaves from Africa to the Americas. 40% went to Brazil, 30% to Cuba, Jamaica and Haiti, and 5% to the USA.

- **The slave trade** involved shipping several hundred thousand Africans across the Atlantic from the 'Slave Coast' of West Africa to the West Indies and the USA, or from Angola to Brazil. Once the slave ships had unloaded their slaves, they would return to Europe with a cargo of sugar, then sail for Africa with cotton goods and guns to exchange for slaves.

> ★ STAR FACT ★
> Conditions on the slave ships were so appalling that 2 million slaves died on them.

- **Slavery was rife** in the American south in the 1700s, where owners of large plantations needed cheap labour to grow first tobacco and then cotton.

- **In the West Indies** and Brazil, there were more blacks than whites and slaves often revolted. The greatest revolution was on French Haiti, where the slave Toussaint l'Ouverture (1743-1803) led 500,000 slaves to take over the country in 1791. For a while Haiti was black-governed – but Napoleon's troops reasserted control in 1802.

- **In the 1790s,** some Europeans began to speak out against slavery. Denmark banned the Atlantic slave trade in 1792. William Wilberforce got Britain to ban the trade in 1807. The USA banned the import of slaves in 1808. When Latin-American countries became independent in the early 1800s, they freed slaves. Britain abolished slavery in its empire in 1833, but the USA had to go through a civil war first.

◀▲ In southern USA many African slaves were field hands, picking cotton (left). Many tried to escape or protest, but they were in a minority – and there was no chance of a revolution like that led by Toussaint l'Ouverture (above) in Haiti.

The Glorious Revolution

- **The Glorious Revolution** of 1688 was when the English parliament replaced James II with William III as king.

- **James II** became king when his brother Charles II died in 1685.

- **James II** was Catholic. He upset people by giving Catholics key jobs in the army, the Church and the universities.

▶ *Mary sided with her Protestant husband, William, against her Catholic father James II.*

- **James II** jailed any bishops who refused to support his Declaration of Indulgence in favour of Catholics.

- **In 1688,** James II and his Catholic wife Mary had a son and it seemed that England was set to become Catholic.

- **Leading Protestants** met and decided to invite the Dutch prince William of Orange to help. William was married to James II's Protestant daughter Mary.

- **William landed** with his army at Brixham in Devon on 5 November 1688. James's army refused to obey its Catholic generals and so he was forced to flee to France.

- **Parliament** decided James's escape meant he had abdicated, and offered the throne to William and Mary.

- **James** tried a comeback, landing in Ulster with French troops. Defeat came at the Battle of the Boyne (July 1689).

> ★ STAR FACT ★
> Ulster Protestants are called Orangemen because they once helped William of Orange at the Boyne.

The Age of Reason

- **The Age of Reason** is the time in the 1700s when many people began to believe that all-important questions about the world could be answered by reason.

- **The Age of Reason** is also called the Enlightenment.

- **The idea that human reason** has the answers was revolutionary. It meant that even the lowliest peasant was just as likely to be right as the highest lord. So why should a lord rule over a peasant?

- **In earlier times,** kings had ruled by 'divine right' – and their power over other people was God's will. The Age of Reason questioned this right.

- **As the 1700s** progressed, the ideas of the Age of Reason turned into real revolutions in France and America.

- **The hero of the Age** was Isaac Newton. His discovery of the Laws of Motion proposed that every single event in the Universe could be worked out mathematically.

- **American revolutionary** leader Jefferson had a portrait of Newton before him as he wrote the Constitution.

- **In France,** the great ideas were worked out by philosophers like Rousseau and Voltaire. People discussed the ideas earnestly at fashionable 'salons' (supper parties).

- **In Britain,** thinkers like Hume showed how important it was to work things out for yourself – not just be told.

- **To sum up all** human knowledge, the first great encyclopedia was created – by Diderot in France.

◀ *Diderot's books showed even everyday processes like glass-making.*

Peter the Great

- **Peter the Great** (1672-1725) was the greatest of all the Russian czars (emperors). He built the city of St Petersburg and turned Russia from an inward-looking country to a major European power.

- **Peter was** well over 2 m tall, and towered above everyone else.

- **Peter had incredible** willpower and a burning interest in new ideas. But he was very impatient and often went into rages. When his son Alexei plotted against him, Peter had him put to death.

◀ *Most earlier czars had bushy, traditional Russian beards. Peter shaved his off, in the European style.*

- **Peter became czar** at the age of ten. His step-sister Sophia ruled for him until 1689, when her enemies drove her out and Peter took charge.

- **In 1697-98** Peter travelled to Holland and England disguised as simple ship's carpenter in order to learn about western European technology and culture.

- **When Peter returned** from Europe, he brought with him many western European craftsmen and teachers.

- **Peter** insisted on Russian men shaving off their old-fashioned, Russian-style beards.

- **Peter** was very keen on boats. He built the first Russian navy – on the Volga River. His wars later ensured that Russia had, for the first time, a sea port on the Baltic.

- **Peter** led the Russian armies to crucial victories in battle – notably against the Swedes at Poltava in 1709.

- **Peter** created the first Russian Academy of Sciences, started Russia's first newspaper, and founded many schools, technical institutions and art galleries.

British India

- **Shortly after** Vasco da Gama reached India, in 1498, the Portuguese set up a trading base in Goa.

- **In 1600,** Elizabeth I of England gave a charter to the East India Co. to trade in India. It set up posts at Surat, Madras, Bombay and Calcutta.

- **The French** set up a base at Pondicherry, in 1668.

- **In the 1700s,** rebellions weakened the Mogul empire. The French and British vied to gain control.

- **In 1757,** 3,000 British soldiers, led by the East India Co.'s Robert Clive, defeated an army of over 50,000 French and Indian troops at the battle of Plassey.

- **After Clive's victory,** the British gradually gained control over much of India through a combination of bribes, bullying and making well-placed allies.

- **In 1803,** the British captured the Mogul capital of Delhi – so completing their power base.

- **In 1858,** the British decided to rule India directly. Their rule was called the Raj (which means 'rule'). In 1876,

▲ *The British did little for farming and industry, but built 55,000 km of railways and grand stations such as this one (in Bombay).*

Queen Victoria of Britain was named empress of India.

- **British rule** was resented by many Indians. Hindus felt that the British were undermining their religion.

- **In 1857,** Indian soldiers revolted and other Indians joined them, but the 'mutiny' was crushed after 14 months.

American independence

◀ **The original 13 colonies of North America** stretched from foggy Massachusetts in the north, 2,500 km south to steamy Georgia. These 13 colonies became the first 13 states of the United States of America. The dates on the map show when they were founded. The green lines show today's states – these, of course, did not exist in 1775. In 1775, there were over 2.5 million people living in the colonies, with 450,000 in Virginia alone.

Map labels:
- Hudson Bay Company
- Maine (part of Massachusetts)
- New Hampshire 1680
- New York 1664
- Massachusetts 1629
- Rhode Island 1635
- Connecticut 1664
- New Jersey 1664
- Pennsylvania 1681
- Delaware 1702
- Maryland 1632
- Indian Reserve
- Virginia 1607
- 1763 Proclamation Line
- N Carolina 1670
- S Carolina 1670
- Georgia 1732
- West Florida
- East Florida

- **In 1763**, Britain finally defeated the French in North America, adding Canada to its 13 colonies – but wanted the colonists to help pay for the cost. The colonists resented paying taxes to a government 5,000 km away.

- **To avoid** costly wars with Native Americans, George III issued a Proclamation in 1763 reserving lands west of the Appalachians for native peoples and sent troops to keep settlers out, arousing the colonists' resentment.

- **In 1764-5**, British Prime Minister Greville brought in three new taxes – the Sugar Tax on molasses, which affected rum producers in the colonies; the Quartering Tax, which obliged the colonists to supply British soldiers with living quarters; and the Stamp Tax on newspapers, playing cards and legal documents.

- **Colonists** tolerated sugar and quartering taxes, but the Stamp Tax provoked riots. Delegates from nine colonies met in New York to demand a say in how they were taxed, demanding 'No taxation without representation.'

- **As protests** escalated, Greville was forced to withdraw all taxes but one, the tax on tea. Then, in 1773, a crowd of colonists disguised as Mohawk Indians marched on to the merchant ship *Dartmouth* in Boston harbour and threw its cargo of tea into the sea. After this 'Boston Tea Party', the British closed Boston and moved troops in.

- **A Congress** of delegates from all the colonies except Georgia met to demand independence, and appointed George Washington to lead an army to fight their cause.

- **In April 1775**, British troops seized military stores at Lexington and Concord near Boston and the war began.

- **At first** the British were successful, but the problems of fighting 5,000 km from home told in the long run. In 1781, Washington defeated the British at Yorktown, Virginia and they surrendered.

- **In 1776**, the colonists drew up a Declaration of Independence, written by Thomas Jefferson. The British recognized independence in 1783, and in 1787 the colonists drew up a Constitution to lay down how their Union should be run. In 1789, George Washington was elected as the first president of the United States of America.

◀ *Thomas Jefferson (1743-1826) was the Virginian who wrote America's Declaration of Independence and became the third US president, in 1801.*

▶ *The American Declaration of Independence of 1776. The 'W' you can see is the first letter of the famous opening words 'We hold these truths...'*

The French Revolution

- **In 1789**, French people were divided among three 'Estates' – the nobles, clergy and middle class – plus the peasants. Nobles owned all the land, but were exempt from paying taxes, and the tax burden fell on the peasants.

- **In 1789**, France was bankrupt after many lost wars, and King Louis XVI was forced to summon Parliament, called the Estates General, for the first time in 175 years.

- **The three Estates** had met separately in the past, but now insisted on meeting in a National Assembly to debate how to limit the power of the king. The Assembly was dominated by the Third Estate, the middle class.

- **On 14 July 1789**, the poor people of Paris, tired of debates, stormed the prison fortress of the Bastille.

- **Fired by the fall** of the Bastille, peasants rose all over the country and refused to pay taxes. Parisian women marched to Versailles and dragged the king back to Paris.

- **The National Assembly** became more radical, ending serfdom and attacking the nobles and the Church. Many nobles fled the country in panic.

◀ *The guillotine had a blade that dropped to cut victims' heads off instantly.*

- **The Assembly** speakers who had the power to move the Paris mobs, like Georges Danton, came to the fore. The Assembly renamed itself the National Convention and set up the Committee of Public Safety to govern France by terror.

- **Many nobles** were sent to the guillotine and in 1793 Louis XVI and his queen, Marie Antoinette, were themselves guillotined.

- **This Reign of Terror** was presided over by Robespierre, who saw more and more of his rivals to the guillotine, including Danton. But in the end even Robespierre himself was guillotined, in July 1794.

- **With Robespierre gone,** conservatives regained control. Emphasis shifted to defending the revolution against foreign kings and to Napoleon's conquests.

Agricultural Revolution

- **The Agricultural Revolution** refers to dramatic changes in farming in Britain in the 1700s and later in the USA.

- **Before the 1700s**, farmland was mostly wide open fields, cultivated in narrow strips by peasants growing food for themselves, using traditional methods.

- **The Agricultural Revolution** created large farms, growing food for profit in small fields, using specialist techniques.

- **The most dramatic effect** was enclosure, in which peasants were evicted from open fields as they were parcelled up into small fields for rearing livestock.

- **Crop-growing** was improved by techniques such as the four-field rotation system.

- **The four-field system** of 'Turnip' Townshend and Thomas Coke meant growing turnips, clover, barley and wheat in successive years so land was used all the time.

- **Livestock farmers** found how to breed cattle, horses and sheep larger and fatter, like Bakewell's Leicester sheep.

- **New machines** were invented. Jethro Tull's drill, for example, made holes and planted seeds in them.

- **In 1793**, Eli Whitney invented a gin machine to separate cotton fibre from the seeds – so making large-scale cotton production possible.

- **In 1834**, American Cyrus McCormick made the first mechanical harvester.

▼ *Bakewell's Leicester sheep made cheap meat widely available.*

Industrial Revolution

▶ In 1764, Lancashire weaver James Hargreaves created the 'spinning jenny' to help cottage weavers spin wool or cotton fibres into yarn (thread) on lots of spindles, turned by a single handle.

- **The Industrial Revolution** refers to the dramatic growth in factories that began in the 1700s.

- **Before the Industrial Revolution**, most ordinary people were farmers living in small villages. Afterwards, most were factory hands and foremen living in huge cities.

- **The Revolution** began in Britain in the late 1700s; in France, the USA and Germany in the early 1800s.

- **The Farming Revolution** created a pool of cheap labour, while the growth of European colonies created vast markets for things like clothing.

- **The Revolution** began with the invention of machines for making cloth, like the spinning jenny.

- **The turning point** was the change from hand-turned machines like the jenny to machines driven by big water wheels – like Arkwright's 'water [-powered spinning] frame' of 1766.

- **In 1771**, Arkwright installed water frames at Crompton Mill, Derby and created the world's first big factory.

- **In the 1780s**, James Watt developed a steam engine to drive machines – and steam engines quickly replaced water as the main source of power in factories.

- **In 1713**, Abraham Darby found how to use coke, rather than wood charcoal, to make huge amounts of iron.

- **In 1784**, Henry Cort found how to remove impurities from cast iron to make wrought iron – and iron became the key material of the Industrial Revolution.

The Jacobites

▶ After 1745, the British banned the wearing of tartan, the Scots' traditional checked cloth.

- **After James II** was deposed as king of England and Scotland in 1688, many Scots still believed he and his Stuart descendants were rightful kings.

- **Supporters** of the Stuarts were called Jacobites after *Jacobus*, Latin for James.

- **James II's** son James was called the Old Pretender, because he pretended to (claimed) the English throne.

- **English Queen Anne** died childless in 1714, and the Scottish and English Jacobites rose in revolt in 1715. This revolution is called 'the Fifteen'.

- **The Old Pretender** arrived in Scotland only after the Fifteen and its leaders had been crushed.

- **The Scots hero** of the Fifteen was Rob Roy MacGregor (1671-1734), an outlaw who stole cattle from English-inclined Duke of Montrose, then joined the rebellion. His tale is told in Walter Scott's novel *Rob Roy* (1817).

- **The Old Pretender's** son Charles was Bonnie Prince Charlie, the Young Pretender.

- **In 1745**, Bonnie Prince Charlie led the Jacobites in a rebellion – called 'the Forty-Five' – against George II.

- **The Jacobites** defeated the English at Prestonpans, then invaded England, advancing as far as Derby before they lost their nerve and retreated.

- **In the sleet**, on bleak Culloden moor near Inverness on 16 April 1746, the Jacobites were routed by the English under the Duke of Cumberland. Cumberland came to be called Butcher, because of the way he ruthlessly hunted down and killed survivors.

Napoleon

◀ *Napoleon, with his right hand hidden, characteristically, inside his jacket.*

- **Napoleon Bonaparte** (1769-1821) was the greatest general of modern times, creating for a short while a French empire that covered most of Europe.

- **Napoleon** was quite short (157 cm) and was nicknamed *le Petit Caporal* ('the tiny corporal'). But he was an inspiring leader, with a genius for planning and an incredibly strong will.

- **Napoleon** was born on the island of Corsica. At the age of nine he went to army school and joined the French army at fourteen.

- **The Revolution** gave Napoleon the chance to shine and by 1794, at just 25, he was a brigadier general.

- **In 1796,** days after marrying Josephine de Beauharnais, Napoleon was sent with a small troop simply to hold up the invading Austrians. Instead, he drove them back as far as Vienna and conquered much of Austria.

- **By 1804,** Napoleon's conquests had made him a hero in France, and the French senate and people elected him as Emperor Napoleon I.

- **By 1812,** Napoleon had defeated all the major countries in Europe but Britain and decided to invade Russia.

- **Napoleon's** invasion of Russia ended in such disaster that it broke his power in Europe. Soon afterwards, he was defeated at Leipzig, Paris was occupied by his enemies and he was sent into exile on the isle of Elba.

- **Napoleon escaped** from Elba in March 1815 to raise another army, but this was defeated by Wellington's armies at Waterloo, Belgium in June.

- **After Waterloo,** Napoleon was sent to the island of St Helena in the mid-Atlantic, where he died, aged 51.

Ireland

- **When the Irish high king,** Turlough O'Connor, overthrew Dermot, the king of Leinster, c.1160, Dermot asked Henry II, the Norman king of England, for help.

- **When Dermot died,** the Norman baron Strongbow made himself king of Leinster. Henry II invaded and Normans slowly gained control of all Ireland.

- **Norman English power** in Ireland weakened as many people adopted Irish ways. By the 1400s, they controlled only a small area round Dublin called the Pale.

- **The phrase 'beyond the Pale'** originally meant the dark and wild Ireland outside the Pale.

- **To regain** control, the English began the 'plantation of Ireland' – giving English settlers land there.

- **In the late 1500s,** the English queen Elizabeth I tried to set up Protestantism in Ireland by force .

- **The Irish** in Ulster revolted, led first by Shane O'Neill and later his nephew Hugh O'Neill, but Elizabeth crushed the rebellion in 1603.

▲ *In July, 1690, Willian III of England fought the former King James II for the English crown at the Battle of the Boyne in Ireland.*

- **Oliver Cromwell** stamped out another Irish revolt in 1649.

- **After the defeat** of James II at the Boyne, Irish Catholics lost more land to English and Irish Protestants. By 1704, they owned just fifteen per cent of Ireland.

- **In 1798,** Wolfe Tone led another Irish revolt – aided by a small French army – but the revolution was soon crushed.

Industrial unrest

> ★ STAR FACT ★
> Thomas Paine's radical book *The Rights of Man* (1792) was the inspiration for many protesters.

- **Wages** in the new factories of the Industrial Revolution were low and working conditions were very poor.

- **Luddites** were English factory workers who, in 1811-12, smashed new machines that put people out of work.

- **High taxes** on imported corn meant that the poor were first to suffer in times of poor harvest, such as 1816-19.

- **The 'Peterloo' massacre** of 16 August 1819 happened when soldiers fired into a crowd gathered to hear radical leader Henry Hunt in Manchester's St Peter's field.

- **Welsh-born Robert Owen** (1771-1858) was the first great factory reformer and socialist.

- **Owen set up** 'ideal' communities at New Lanark in Scotland and New Harmony in Indiana, USA, where people might work together in good conditions.

▶ GWM Reynolds was one of the leaders of the Chartists, the first great working class movement.

- **Trade unions** were banned by British 'Combination' Acts. But these were partly removed in 1824.

- **Owen's** Grand National Consolidated Trades Union of 1833 – the first national union – was instantly repressed by the government.

- **The Tolpuddle martyrs** were six Dorset farmworkers transported to Australia in 1834 for simply meeting up.

Austria and Prussia

▶ As well as being a ruthless military leader, Frederick the Great played and composed flute music and exchanged long letters with the philosopher Voltaire.

- **In 1711,** Austria, Hungary, Germany and Italy were part of the Holy Roman Empire. The Emperor was Charles VI, the Archduke of Austria.

- **Charles VI** had no sons, but wanted his young daughter Maria Theresa to rule after him.

- **When Charles VI died, in 1740,** three non-Austrians claimed they should be Emperor. Maria Theresa rallied her Austrian people to defend her claim.

- **The War of the Austrian Succession** began with Britain, Hungary and the Netherlands backing Maria Theresa. Prussia, France, Bavaria, Saxony, Sardinia and Spain opposed her.

- **In 1742,** Maria Theresa was defeated and Charles of Bavaria became emperor. Charles, however, died in 1745. Maria Theresa's husband Francis I became emperor, though Maria was actually in charge.

- **The rise of Prussia** is linked to the rise of their ruling family the Hohenzollerns, and aristocratic landlords called junkers.

- **In 1417,** Frederick Hohenzollern became elector of Brandenburg. This meant he was one of the chosen few who could elect the Holy Roman Emperor.

- **By 1701,** Brandenburg expanded to become Prussia. Frederick I became its first king and built up its army.

- **Frederick I's son,** Frederick II or Frederick the Great (1712-86), was Prussia's greatest ruler. Frederick II was ambitious and manoeuvred Austria, France and Russia into wars that he used to gain land.

- **Austria and Prussia** lost much of their power after they were beaten by Napoleon's armies.

Napoleonic Wars

▶ This map shows some of the major battles of the Napoleonic Wars.

- **The Napoleonic Wars** were the long and bitter wars (1796-1815) between the France of Napoleon and other European countries, including Britain.

- **The wars began** with Napoleon scoring decisive victories over the Austrians in northern Italy in 1796 .

- **Napoleon** wanted to destroy British trade with the Middle East, and so attacked Egypt in 1798, defeating Egypt's rulers the Mamelukes – by the pyramids near Cairo. Napoleon's fleet was destroyed on the Nile by the British under Lord Nelson, but Napoleon then beat the Turks at Abuqir and went home in glory and triumph to be elected emperor.

- **The French Revolution** had introduced a conscript system, which meant that every Frenchman had to serve in the army – Napoleon's army was 750,000 in 1799. Two million more had joined up by 1815.

- **In 1805**, Britain, Russia and Austria allied against Napoleon. Napoleon crushed the Austrians and Russians at Austerlitz. When Prussia joined Russia the next year, Napoleon routed the Prussians at Jena and Auerstadt and the Russians at Friedland. But in 1805 Nelson's ships had destroyed the French fleet at Trafalgar, off Spain. Nelson died at Trafalgar, but his victory ended Napoleon's chances of invading Britain.

> ★ STAR FACT ★
> Napoleon won many victories by holding much of his army in reserve until he had opened up a carefully chosen weak point in enemy lines.

- **A key element** in the French success was the 'column'. Instead of advancing in a thin line, men marched almost up to the enemy in columns, then quickly spread out.

- **Napoleon** tried to destroy Britain with the 'Continental System', which banned any country from trading with it. This damaged British trade but cost Napoleon support.

- **In 1812**, Napoleon marched into Russia and captured Moscow, but the Russians burned everything as they fell back – leaving the French without food. Napoleon had to retreat from Moscow in the bitterest winter.

- **After the 1812 disaster**, Napoleon's enemies moved in swiftly. After a crushing defeat at Leipzig, Napoleon abdicated, his enemies occupied Paris and he went into exile on Elba. His brief comeback in 1815 ended in defeat at Waterloo.

◀ Napoleon's retreat from Moscow in 1812 was one of the worst of all military disasters. The winter trek was so cold and food so scarce that only 30,000 of the army of 695,000 that set out made it back to France.

The Year of revolutions

▶ When rioters raged through Vienna, the feared Prince Metternich and many of his hated secret police were forced to flee.

- **The year 1848** saw revolutions break out right across Europe – in France, Germany, Italy, Austria and Hungary.

- **The revolutions** were not linked directly, but the revolutionaries had many of the same grievances.

- **Most revolutionaries** were also angry at repressive governments in which too few had a say.

- **Many revolutionaries** were angry too at the poverty suffered by ordinary people in the new industrial cities.

- **Many places**, like Hungary, Germany and Italy, were under the power of a foreign government, and revolutionaries were often nationalists who wanted freedom from foreign oppression for their country.

- **In Paris**, revolutionaries shouting 'bread or death' stormed government buildings, threw out the king and set up a republic.

- **In Vienna**, the powerful Prince Metternich and emperor were forced to flee as people created their own parliament and freed serfs.

- **In Hungary**, revolutionary leader Louis Kossuth set up a short-lived Hungarian republic.

- **In London**, the last and biggest Chartist rally took place. The Chartists had a charter demanding votes for all men and other political reforms. The rally dispersed peacefully.

- **All but the Paris Revolution** were quickly dealt with by armies – but the desire for change grew stronger over the century. The *Communist Manifesto*, written by Karl Marx and Friedrich Engels, was to become the basis of the great revolutions in Russia and China.

Latin American revolts

- **By 1800**, Latin Americans were ready to revolt against the centuries of rule by Spain and Portugal.

- **When the Napoleonic Wars** turned Spain and Portugal into a battleground, Latin American revolutionaries seized their chance.

- **Mexicans** led by priests Hidalgo and Morelos revolted in 1810. The Spanish quelled the revolt and executed Hidalgo and Morelos. In 1821, however, Mexico gained independence.

- **In 1810**, José de San Martin led Argentina to independence. In 1816, San Martin made an epic march across the Andes to bring Chile freedom, too – with the help of Bernardo O'Higgins.

◀ Simon Bolivar (1783-1830) was South America's greatest revolutionary hero, but as president of Gran Colombia he proved unpopular.

> **★ STAR FACT ★**
> In 1824, San Martin left for Europe, saddened by disputes after independence and his wife's death.

- **In the north,** Venezuelans Francisco de Miranda, Simon Bolivar and Antonio de Sucre led a long fight against the Spanish in New Granada (now Colombia) and Peru. In 1819, after a great victory at Boyaca in Colombia, Bolivar proclaimed the Republic of Gran Colombia (now Venezuela, Colombia, Ecuador and Panama).

- **In 1824**, Sucre won a crucial victory at Ayacucho in Peru, freeing all of north South America from Spanish rule.

- **The Republic** of Bolivia was named after Bolivar, who wrote its constitution. Sucre became its first president.

- **Brazil** gained its freedom from Portugal without a fight when its ruler Prince John fled. His son became emperor.

- **Miranda** died in a Spanish jail after Bolivar handed him over. Sucre was assassinated in 1830. Bolivar died in 1830, shortly after a failed assassination attempt.

Italian independence

▶ Garibaldi was the hero who landed in Italy with just his thousand famous 'Red Shirts', formed to fight for freedom in Uruguay. He went on to conquer all of southern Italy.

- **After the Napoleonic Wars**, Italy was split into various kingdoms – some, like Naples, under French Bourbon kings, some under Austrian rule and papal states under the pope.

- **The Carbonari** ('charcoal burners') were a secret society working for Italian freedom.

- **In 1820**, the Carbonari got the Bourbon king of Naples to agree to a constitution, but the Austrians stamped on it.

- **In 1831**, Giuseppe Mazzini founded 'Young Italy' to unite Italy. The drive to unite the country became known as the *Risorgimento* ('rising again').

- **In 1848**, revolutions broke out across Italy, but were put down.

- **In 1857**, Count Cavour, prime minister of Piedmont, asked France for help with evicting the Austrians.

- **In 1859**, France and Piedmont beat the Austrians at Magenta and Solferino. After political wrangling, northern Italy was joined to Piedmont under King Victor Emmanuel II.

- **Magenta** was such a bloody battle that a new purple-red colour was named after it.

- **In 1860**, the great hero Garibaldi led a rebellion and conquered all of southern Italy. Only Cavour's intervention stopped Garibaldi from taking Rome.

- **In 1861**, most of Italy was united under Victor Emmanuel. Venice was added in 1866 and Rome as capital in 1870.

The Irish famine

- **The Irish potato famine** (1845-49) was one of the worst human disasters of the 1800s, when more than a million people in Ireland died of starvation.

- **In the 1800s**, most Irish were poor farmers, working tiny plots of land rented from Anglo-Irish landlords.

- **Potatoes were introduced** from America in the 1700s. They were such a successful crop that the Irish population

grew to 8.4 million by 1844, but most were very poor.

- **Half the Irish** population depended entirely on potatoes for food, because English laws kept the price of bread too high for the poor Irish to buy.

- **In 1845**, much of the potato crop was ruined by blight, a disease caused by the fungus *Phytophthora*.

- **When the blight** ruined even more of the 1846-49 potato crops, millions of poor Irish farmers began to starve.

- **By August 1847**, three million were fed entirely on rations from soup kitchens set up by landlords and the British.

- **Many poor tenant farmers** were thrown off their land because they had no crop to sell in order to pay the rent.

- **Throughout the famine**, Irish farms exported grain, meat and vegetables too costly for the Irish to buy.

- **One and a half million** desperate Irish people packed up and left for America, leaving the country half-empty.

◀ The potato famine devastated Ireland.

The British Empire

★ STAR FACT ★
In 1920, 600 million people around the world were ruled from London.

- **At its height**, in 1920, the British Empire covered a quarter of the world and ruled a quarter of the world's population.

- **The British** settled in more lands and ruled more peoples than any other nation in history.

- **The British Empire** began to build up in the 1600s, as British merchants started to extend their trading links throughout the world. The British won out over Dutch, Portuguese, French and Belgian rivals through the success of their navy and also their reasonably efficient colonial government.

- **The 13 American colonies** broke away in 1776, but Canada and many West Indian islands remained British.

- **Britain** gained control of India through the East India Company, between 1757 and 1858. In 1877, Queen Victoria was proclaimed Empress of India – the first time the word empire had been used in relation to the British possessions.

- **Many of the British possessions** had similar climates to Britain's – parts of Canada, South Africa, Australia and New Zealand – and British settlers moved to these places in huge numbers in the 1900s, pushing out the native inhabitants. These colonies were given more and more freedom to govern themselves and came to be called 'dominions'.

- **The Empire** reached its peak after World War 1, when German and Turkish possessions were added.

- **After World War 2**, more and more countries – especially in India and Africa – demanded independence. India and Pakistan became independent in 1947, Ceylon in 1948. By 1980, most African, West Indian and Pacific Island colonies also gained independence.

- **Most colonies** remained within the Commonwealth of Nations after independence. There are 54 Commonwealth nations, now linked essentially by agreed principles, but they all accept the British queen as head of the Commonwealth.

▲ The British Empire was kept under control both by the British Royal Navy, which commanded the seas, and the British army. The army, with its familiar red uniforms, were at work in every continent in the world, from India to Egypt, and Australia to Canada.

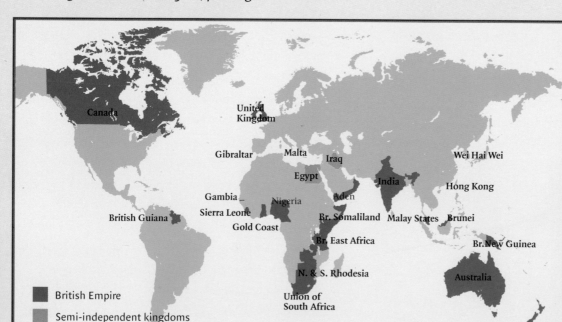

◄ This map shows the British Empire in the 1930s, when it was already beginning to shrink. Egypt was given some independence in 1922, when Sultan Ahmed became King Fuad I. Iraq gained a similar independence when amir Ahd Allah Faisal became King Faisal I.

Canada
United Kingdom
Gibraltar
Malta
Iraq
Egypt
Wei Hai Wei
India
Hong Kong
Gambia
Nigeria
Aden
Sierra Leone
Br. Somaliland
Malay States
Brunei
British Guiana
Gold Coast
Br. East Africa
Br. New Guinea
N. & S. Rhodesia
Australia
Union of South Africa
New Zealand
Falklands

■ British Empire
■ Semi-independent kingdoms

The American Civil War

- **The American Civil War** (1861-65) was fought between northern states (the Union) and southern states (the Confederacy). It split friends and families and killed over 600,000 Americans.

- **The main cause** was slavery. In 1850, slavery was banned in the 18 northern states, but there were 4 million slaves in the 15 southern states, where they worked on huge plantations.

- **The conflicts developed** over whether new states, added as settlers pushed westward, should be 'slave' or 'free' states.

- **In 1854**, slavers gained legal victories with the Kansas-Nebraska Act, which let new states decide for themselves.

- **In 1860**, the Abolitionist (anti-slavery) Republican, Abraham Lincoln, was elected as president.

- **The southern states** immediately broke away from the Union in protest, to form their own Confederacy.

◀ *The Union flag had stars for all the 13 original states (top). The Confederates had their own version of the flag, also with 13 stars.*

- **As the war began,** the Confederates had the upper hand, fighting a defensive campaign.

- **The turning point** came in July 1863, when an invading southern army, commanded by Robert E Lee, was badly defeated at Gettysburg in Pennsylvania.

- **The extra** industrial resources of the north slowly began to tell and General Grant attacked the south from the north, while Sherman advanced ruthlessly from the west.

- **Lee surrendered** to Grant in Appomattox Court House, Virginia, on 9 April 1865. Slavery was abolished, but a few days later Lincoln was assassinated.

Australia

- **In 1788**, the British sent a fleet of 11 ships, carrying convicts, to start a prison colony in Australia.

- **The fleet landed** at Botany Bay, but the first governor, Arthur Phillip, settled in a new site that eventually became the city of Sydney.

- **160,000 convicts** were sent to Australia over the next 80 years, but by 1810 British settlers were arriving voluntarily.

- **After 1850**, settlers set up vast sheep farms in the interior. Many Aborigines were killed as they fought for their land.

▼ *In 1770, Captain James Cook landed on the east coast of Australia and claimed it for Britain.*

- **In 1851**, gold was discovered in New South Wales and Victoria and many thousands of people came to Australia to seek their fortune, tripling the population to 1.1 million in just nine years.

- **After the gold rushes**, ex-miners campaigned to 'unlock the lands' – that is, free up land from squatters and landowners for small farmers.

- **In the 1880s and 90s**, Australians began to become aware of their own national identity – partly as Australian cricketers became heroes – and demand self-government.

- **In 1901**, Australia became the independent Commonwealth of Australia, with its own parliament at Melbourne.

- **In 1927**, the Australian government moved to a new capital in Canberra.

- **In 2000**, Australians voted to keep the British queen as head of state, rather than become a republic.

The scramble for Africa

- **From 1500 to 1800**, Europeans were familiar only with the coast of Africa, from which slaves were taken.

- **After 1800**, many Europeans wanted to explore the interior in order to spread Christianity.

- **Some Europeans** wanted to develop trade in products like minerals and palm oil to help combat the slave trade.

- **Many European explorers**, such as David Livingstone and Richard Burton, went to Africa to find out more about its 'dark' (unknown) interior.

- **The wealth brought** to Britain by its colonies, such as India and North America, spurred the European powers to look for more lands to colonize.

- **In the 1880s**, Europeans competed fiercely for African colonies. This feverish competition was called 'the scramble for Africa'.

- **By 1920**, Belgium, France, Germany, Great Britain, Italy, Portugal and Spain had divided all of Africa between them.

Belgian
French
Italian
German
Spanish
Portuguese
British
Independent

Rio de Oro
Libya (1912)
Egypt (1882)
French W. Africa (1876-98)
Sudan (1898)
Somaliland (1889-92)
Liberia
Nigeria (1884-1900)
Ethiopia
Br E. Africa (1886)
Congo (1885)
German E. Africa (1886)
Angola
SW Africa (1884)
Madagascar (1895-96)
SW Africa (1884)

▶ The European colonies in Africa in 1900, and the dates they were acquired.

- **In some parts** of Africa, colonial rule was established peacefully by agreement with the Africans.

- **In Nigeria** and Ghana, the Africans fought hard against British rule, and in Tanzania and Namibia, they fought against German rule.

- **Ethiopia and** Liberia were the only countries in Africa to hold on to their independence.

The Oregon trail

- **After the USA** became independent, in 1783, waves of settlers began to move westward.

- **The first settlers** were fur traders. These were followed by cattle ranchers, then other farmers.

- **When cattle ranchers** moved to the Great Plains, they grazed huge herds on the open range and drove them to newly built rail depots for shipment east.

- **The cattle ranchers** of the Great Plains employed cowboys to herd the cattle and these cowboys became the symbol of the American west.

- **As the settlers** pushed west they came into conflict with Native Americans who already lived there.

- **The settlers** made many treaties with local peoples but broke almost all of them, and Native Americans were gradually driven from their lands or simply slaughtered.

- **In each decade**, new settlers struggled further west, facing great hardship in the hope of finding a new life.

- **Settlers** often set out with all their possessions in a covered wagon, often travelling with other wagons in a train (convoy) for safety.

- **The Oregon trail** was the longest of the routes to the west, winding over 3,000 km from Independence, Missouri to the Pacific northwest.

- **The first group** of 900 wagons set out on the Oregon trail in the Great Migration of 1843.

◀ Would-be settlers packed everything they had in a covered wagon and joined a train heading west.

The Crimean War

- **The Crimean War** was fought in the Crimea – to the north of the Black Sea – between 1854 and 1856.

- **On one side** was Russia. On the other were Turkey, Britain, Piedmont/Sardinia and Austria.

- **The main cause** of the war was British, French and Turkish worries about Russian expansion in the Black Sea.

- **The war began** when Russia destroyed the Turkish fleet.

- **Armies on both sides** were badly organized. Many British soldiers died of cholera before they even reached the Crimea and wounded soldiers suffered badly from cold and disease.

▲ 250 of the 670 cavalrymen of the Light Brigade died in their heroic but useless charge.

- **During the Battle of Balaklava**, on 25 October 1854, a stupid mistake sent a gallant British cavalry charge straight on to the Russian guns. The heroic 'Charge of the Light Brigade' was made famous in a poem by Tennyson.

- **Conditions** in the battle hospitals were reported in the first-ever war photographs and in the telegraphed news reports of W H Russell.

- **Nurses** like Florence Nightingale and Jamaican Mary Seacole went to the Crimea to help the wounded.

- **Lessons learned** in the Crimea helped to lay the foundations of modern nursing.

- **The war** finally ended in 1856 with the Treaty of Paris, with few gains on either side.

Germany

- **In 1815**, Germany was divided among 38 different states of the German Confederation.

- **The most powerful** of the German states were Prussia and Austria, who sparred for dominance.

- **In 1862**, Otto von Bismarck (1815-98) became chancellor of Prussia. He was known as 'the Iron Chancellor' and it was through his determination and skilful diplomacy that Germany was united.

- **In 1864**, Denmark tried to take over the disputed duchies of Schleswig and Holstein. The Austrians and Prussians sent an army to drive the Danes out.

- **Austria and Prussia** could not agree on what to do with Schleswig-Holstein.

- **Bismarck** proposed a new North German Confederation, excluding Austria.

- **Austria objected** to Bismarck's plan, but was defeated by Prussia in a very swift war in 1866.

- **To complete** Prussian control over Germany, Bismarck

provoked a war against France, which had been the main opponent to German unity. He used the trick of the Ems telegram – a version of a telegram reporting a conversation between the Prussian king and the French ambassador, skilfully edited to imply an insult to France.

- **France** declared war on Prussia, but was swiftly beaten by the Prussians, who marched into Paris in January 1871.

- **After the defeat** of France, all the German states agreed to become part of a united Germany under Prussian leadership. On 18 January 1871, Wilhelm I was crowned kaiser (emperor).

▶ Otto von Bismarck was the tough Prussian chancellor who engineered German unity.

The rise of America

The President and Executive in the White House prepares laws and puts them into effect – and also conducts foreign affairs – but only Congress can make laws legal.

The Congress is the legislative body – the lawmakers. It meets in Washington's Capitol building and is split into two bodies: the House of Representatives and the Senate. There are 100 Senators (two from each state), elected for six years, and 435 Representatives or 'Congressmen', elected in batches every two years.

The Supreme Court is the judiciary, which decides how laws should be applied, and whether laws are acceptable by the Constitution. The nine judges meet in the Supreme Court building.

● **In the late 1800s**, the USA changed from a nation of farming pioneers and plantation owners to the world's biggest industrial powerhouse. American inventors and industrialists made products that changed the world – the typewriter (1867), the telephone (1876), the phonograph (1877) and electric light (1879). Then, in the early 1900s, Henry Ford pioneered the mass production of cars and made cars affordable for millions of ordinary people.

● **The writer** Mark Twain called the era of industrialization 'the Gilded Age', to describe the culture of the newly rich. Without any traditions of their own to draw on, they developed a showy culture aping that of European aristocrats – going to operas and building enormous European-style mansions filled with antiques, works by European painters and rare books.

> ★ **STAR FACT** ★
> By 1930, Americans owned 23 million cars –
> three times as many as the rest of the world.

◀ The Constitution of 1787 split the government of the USA into three arms, to prevent any part becoming too powerful: the President and Executive, Congress and the Supreme Court.

● **The less rich** enjoyed different kinds of show – circuses, vaudevilles and sport. By 1900, baseball was the national pastime. After 1920, motion pictures drew millions.

● **In the late 1800s,** many people started to realize that American progress was leaving many behind, and reformers called Progressives began to demand change. In 1891, farmers and labourers formed the Populist party.

● **In 1903,** Theodore Roosevelt was elected as president and promised Americans a 'square deal'. He tried to curb the power of monopolies like Standard Oil and supported striking miners.

● **Until 1900,** the USA played little part in world affairs. Bismarck said, 'A special Providence takes care of fools, drunkards and the USA'. But in 1898, the US battleship *Maine* was blown up off Cuba. Americans blamed the Spanish and in the war that followed, the USA easily defeated Spain.

● **From 1900 on**, the USA became more and more involved in world affairs, stepping in later in both World War 1 and World War 2 to play a decisive role. By the late 1900s, the USA saw itself to some extent as the world's policeman.

● **By the 1920s,** America was booming. The 1920s were known as the Roaring Twenties, because the pace of change was so exciting, and cars and loud jazz music made the new America so noisy and vibrant.

● **The confidence** of the 1920s spurred wild speculation on money markets, and in 1929 New York's Wall Street stock market crashed. US economic power was now so great that the crash plunged the world into the Great Depression of the 1930s, which saw businesses fold and millions unemployed.

▶ When Franklin D. Roosevelt (1882-1945) was elected President in 1932 one in four Americans were unemployed, many families too poor to eat and 5,000 banks had failed. He promised a New Deal. Remarkably, it worked.

Victorian England

- **In 1837**, 18-year-old Victoria became the queen of England and reigned for 63 years until 1901 – the longest reign in British history.

- **Victoria's reign** is called the Victorian Age.

- **In the Victorian Age**, Britain became the world's largest industrial and trading power and the British Empire reached its peak.

- **British factories and towns** mushroomed and railways were built throughout the country.

- **In 1851**, the Great Exhibition opened in a huge building of glass and iron, later called the Crystal Palace, to show British skills to the world.

- **In 1861**, Victoria's husband, Prince Albert, died and she went into mourning and wore black the rest of her life.

◀ Six million people visited the Great Exhibition in London in 1851.

- **The rapid expansion** of Victorian cities created vast slum areas where living conditions were appalling.

- **Social reformers** and writers such as Charles Dickens highlighted the problems of the slums. Slowly, parliament passed laws to improve conditions for working people and to provide education for all.

- **The two great** prime ministers of the Victorian Age were the flamboyant Benjamin Disraeli (1804-81) and the dour William Gladstone (1809-98).

- **Victorian middle-class life** cultivated cosy moral values, but there was also a seamy side, with widespread prostitution and crime.

The Balkans

- **The Balkans** are the countries of southeastern Europe. The word *balkan* is Turkish for 'mountain'.

- **In 1800**, people of many nationalities lived in the Balkans – Slovenes, Croats, Serbs, Bulgars, Greeks and Turks.

- **All the Balkan peoples** were ruled over by two old and weak empires – Austria-Hungary and Ottoman Turkey.

- **Through the 1800s**, many nationalities in the Balkans worked for independence.

- **European powers** like Russia and Germany encouraged independence movements for their own purposes.

- **Between 1829 and 1908**, Greece, Montenegro, Serbia, Romania and Bulgaria gained some independence, but many of their people were still in the old empires.

- **Austria refused** Slovenia and Croatia independence and held on to Bosnia-Herzegovina, which Serbia claimed.

- **In 1912**, various Balkan countries conspired to drive the Turks out of Europe in the First Balkan War, but rivalry between them led to a Second Balkan War in 1913, which

◀ Within just four days after the assassination of Archduke Franz Ferdinand, World War 1 had started.

let the Turks back in and left the Balkans highly unstable.

- **In June 1914**, Archduke Franz Ferdinand was assassinated in Sarajevo by Gavrilo Princip, a Serbian activist from Bosnia-Herzegovina.

- **Austria** believed Serbs were behind the assassination and declared war. Russia defended the Serbs as they had pledged by secret treaty. Soon all of Europe was engaged in World War 1.

The Opium Wars

▲ Millions of Chinese became addicted to opium in the early 1800s.

- **From 1759 to 1842,** Chinese emperors let European merchants trade only in the port of Guangzhou, and buy tea and silk only from the *cohong* (guild) of Chinese firms.

- **To pay for Chinese goods,** the East India Company used opium, the drug made from poppies. Huge loads of opium grown in India were sold to Chinese drug dealers.

- **All the silver** used to pay for opium upset the Chinese economy and opium-smuggling got out of hand.

- **In March 1839,** Chinese commissioner Lin Tse-hsü seized 20,000 crates of opium from British merchants.

- **Many ordinary** Chinese backed the British, because the British gave them opium and because the emperor's restrictive rule had brought poverty and hunger.

- **In 1840,** 16 British warships went to Guangzhou, starting the First Opium War. The Chinese were easily beaten.

- **Under the Treaty of Nanjing** in 1842, the Chinese gave Britain Hong Kong, abolished the cohong system and opened up trade to specially favoured nations.

- **In 1856,** Chinese police seized the *Arrow,* a ship flying a British flag, thus starting the Second Opium War.

- **British and French** armies invaded China and, after some wrangling, occupied Beijing in 1860.

- **At the Beijing Convention,** China opened more ports to western trade and allowed Europeans to travel inland.

Abraham Lincoln

- **Abraham Lincoln** (1809–65) was America's 16th, and possibly greatest, president. He led the Union through the Civil War and the freeing of slaves.

- **He was born** in a backwoods log cabin in Kentucky, to a poor family.

- **He never went** to school but a relative said, "I never seen Abe after twelve 'at he didn't have a book in his hand or his pocket" – often the Bible.

- **He became a lawyer,** known for shrewd common sense and honesty. His defence of Rock Island Bridge (on the Mississippi River) against shipping interests made him famous.

- **Once elected** to Congress, he went on to win political fame as an opponent of slavery through debates over the Kansas-Nebraska Act, in the 1850s.

▲ Lincoln was a tall, lanky man. His razor-sharp mind, calm manner and resolutely moral attitudes made him a hero to many Americans.

- **In 1860,** just before the start of the Civil War ,between north and south, he was elected president – on the votes of the northern states alone.

- **On 1 January 1863,** Lincoln announced his Emancipation Proclamation, which freed all slaves.

- **In 1863,** after the terrible battle of Gettysburg, Lincoln made a famous speech called the Gettysburg Address, which summed up the spirit of democracy. In it he vowed that 'government of the people, by the people, for the people, shall not perish from the Earth.'

- **When the war** ended, in 1865, he made plans for peaceful reconciliation.

- **He was shot dead** at Ford's Theatre, Washington by John Wilkes Booth, a fanatical southerner.

The Second Empire

- **In the 1840s**, the poverty of workers in French towns inspired men like Proudhon and Fourier to devise socialist ideas for solving various social problems.

- **Political meetings** were banned, so agitators held banquets to press their demands for liberal reforms.

- **On 22 February 1848**, the government banned a huge banquet in Paris, provoking such protest and rioting that King Louis-Philippe was forced to abdicate.

- **After much wrangling**, a new popular assembly set up the Second Republic and Louis-Napoleon Bonaparte was elected president in a vote by all French men.

- **Louis-Napoleon** (1808-73) was the son of Napoleon's brother and his step-daughter Hortense. In his youth, he had been active in the Italian Carbonari.

> ★ STAR FACT ★
> The famous boulevards of Paris, with their grand houses, were created on Napoleon III's orders.

- **The Assembly** proved conservative and, in 1852, Louis-Napoleon curbed their powers and had himself made Emperor Napoleon III by popular vote. His rule is called the Second Empire.

- **Napoleon III** gave state aid to industry, banks and railroads. Industry boomed and France grew rich. French engineers became world-famous.

- **Napoleon III's** Spanish wife, Eugenie, set the Empire Style for beautiful, lavish fashions and decoration that was mimicked across Europe.

- **Gradually**, Napoleon's rule provoked more and more hostility among radicals, and France's defeat by Germany in 1871 led to his downfall.

▶ Radical politicians came to the fore in the Empire.

The Russian Revolution

- **In 1861**, Czar Alexander II freed Russian serfs, but they stayed poor. In towns, factory workers were just as poor.

- **Unrest among** factory workers and peasants grew and by 1901 there were two revolutionary parties: Socialist Revolutionary (SRP) and Socialist Democrat (SDP).

- **In 1903**, the SDP split into *Bolsheviks* (extremist majority), led by Lenin, and *Mensheviks* (moderate minority).

- **In 1905**, after Russia's disastrous war against Japan, workers and peasants rose in revolt and workers from arms factories set up the first *soviets* (workers' councils).

- **Czar Nicholas II** was forced to set up a *Duma* (parliament) but soon began to ignore it.

- **In March 1917**, terrible losses among Russian soldiers in World War 1, plus hardship at home, provoked a revolution.

- **The first 1917** revolution is called the February Revolution, because this was the month in the old Russian calendar.

- **Czar Nicholas** abdicated. Later, the Bolsheviks probably shot him and all his family at Ykaterinburg.

- **The SRP**, led by Kerensky, had the upper hand at first, but more soviets were set up and Bolseheviks gained support.

- **On 7 November** (25 October on the old calendar), the Bolsheviks seized the Winter Palace in St Petersburg. Lenin headed a new government, based in Moscow, and ended the war, while soviets took control of major cities.

▼ The Russian Revolution reached a climax when the Bolsheviks stormed the Winter Palace in St Petersburg.

World War 1

◀ Trenches were dug to protect troops from enemy gunfire, but soon became muddy hell-holes, filled with water, rats and disease. Soldiers had to eat, sleep and stand guard ankle-deep in mud. Every now and then, they were ordered by officers to 'go over the top' – climb out of their trenches and advance towards enemy lines. Once out of the trench, they were completely exposed to enemy fire, and quickly mown down. Millions of soldiers on both sides died this way. On 1 July 1916, 60,000 British soldiers were killed in just a few hours in the Battle of the Somme. The four-month Somme offensive killed 600,000 Germans, 400,000 British and 200,000 French – and advanced the Allies just 7 km. The horror of war in the trenches was conveyed in letters home and in poems by soldiers such as Siegfried Sassoon and Wilfred Owen.

- **World War 1** (1914-18), the Great War, was the worst the world had seen (World War 2 would prove to be worse), killing ten million troops and involving many countries.

- **The war was caused** by the intense rivalry between European powers in the early 1900s. The trigger was the assassination of Franz Ferdinand in Sarajevo, Balkans, on 28 June 1914. This made Austria start a war with Serbia and Russia came to Serbia's defence. Germany declared war on Russia and Russia's ally France on 3 August.

- **The Germans** had a secret plan (the 'Schlieffen plan') for invading France – and put it into action on 4 August. Instead of tackling the French head-on, as expected, they swept round to the north through neutral Belgium. The outrage to Belgium drew Britain into the war.

- **As the Germans** moved on into France, they came up against the British and French (the Allies). The opposing armies dug defensive trenches – and stayed facing each other in much the same place for the whole four years of the war. The line of trenches, known as the Western front, soon stretched from the English Channel to Switzerland.

- **The war soon** developed an Eastern front, where the Central Powers (Austria and Germany) faced the Russians. This front, too, became bogged down. The deaths of millions of Russians provoked the 1917 Revolution, which took Russia out of the war.

- **In the Alps** the Central Powers were opposed by Italy, while at Gallipoli in Turkey, British and Anzac (Australia and New Zealand) troops fought the Turks.

- **The Allies** relied on supplies from N. America, so the Germans used U-boats (submarines) to attack ships in the Atlantic. The sinking of the liner *Lusitania* in May 1915, with 128 Americans out of 1,198 casualties, helped bring the USA decisively into the war in 1917 against Germany.

- **In 1918** there were 3.5 million Germans on the Western front and in March they broke through towards Paris.

- **In July** British tanks broke the German line at Amiens.

- **An Allied naval blockade** meant many people were starving in Germany. As more US troops arrived, the Germans were pushed back. At 11 o'clock on 11 November 1918, the Germans signed an armistice (peace).

The Ottoman Empire

- **In 1774**, the Turkish Ottoman Empire was defeated by the Russians after a six-year war, and was forced to allow Russian ships to pass through the Straits from the Black Sea to the Mediterranean.

- **During the 1800s**, the Ottoman Empire grew weaker and weaker and was called 'the Sick Man of Europe' by foreign statesmen.

- **In 1829**, the Greeks fought a successful war of independence against the Turks. Other Balkan states followed suit.

- **During the 1800s**, the Turks fought four wars against Russia and lost three. Russia gained Bessarabia (now Moldova and Ukraine) and control of the Black Sea.

▲ *Janissaries were the flamboyant elite soldiers of the Ottoman Empire. They were originally prisoners of war.*

- **Trying to stop** the empire's decline, Sultan Abdul-Hamid II crushed opposition violently in the 1890s.

- **The Young Turks** were students and army officers who, in 1908, revolted against Abdul-Hamid and then ruled through his brother Muhammad V.

- **The Turks** joined World War 1 on the German side to regain territory lost to the Russians and in the Balkans.

- **After World War 1** ended, the Allies invaded Turkey and broke up the empire, leaving just modern Turkey.

- **The nationalist hero** Mustafa Kemal became first president of the Turkish republic, on 29 October 1923.

- **Kemal** became known as Ataturk (father of the Turks). He used his great power to weaken the hold of Islam.

The rise of the Nazis

- **Even before** World War 1 ended, Germans had risen in revolt against their kaiser (emperor), Wilhelm II.

- **Wilhelm II** was driven out and in 1919 Germany became a republic, with a president elected by the people.

- **The republic** was called the Weimar Republic, because the parliament met in Weimar.

- **Under the peace terms** for World War 1, Germany was forced to pay huge amounts of money for war damage.

- **The cost of the war** ruined the German economy and rapidly rising prices made people poor overnight.

- **In 1923**, the National Socialist German Workers Party – Nazis – led by Adolf Hitler, tried a rebellion in Munich. The rebellion failed, but support for the Nazis grew.

- **The Great Depression** threw half the German population out of work, and in 1933 enough people voted for the Nazis to make them the strongest party in parliament. Hitler became chancellor and at once set about destroying the opposition.

▶ *To boost their support, the Nazis held huge meetings called rallies, at which their cross symbol, the swastika, was prominently displayed.*

- **The Nazis** asserted German superiority over other races, including Jews and Slavs. They removed Jews from all government jobs and took away their rights.

- **On 9 Nov 1938**, Nazis broke windows and burned down synagogues and Jewish businesses. This night became known as *Kristallnacht* ('Night of the Broken Glass').

- **The Nazis** prepared for war to give Germans *Lebensraum* ('living space'). In 1936, they marched into the Rhineland, lost after World War 1. In 1938, they took Austria, followed by Czechoslovakia in 1939, and then Poland.

Lenin and Stalin

- **Lenin** (1870-1924) was the leader of the Communist revolution in Russia.

- **Lenin's real name** was Vladimir Ilich Ulyanov. He took the name Lenin from the River Lena in Siberia when he became a revolutionary.

- **Like Karl Marx** (1818-83), Lenin believed the world's workers would revolt and take over industry. Unlike Marx, he thought a small band of professionals like the Bolsheviks would need to lead the way.

- **After the 1905** revolution, Lenin lived in exile, but he returned to Russia when the czar fell, in 1917.

- **After the October Revolution,** Lenin ruled the country as head of the Bolsheviks (now the Communists). The Communists won the civil war that followed and in 1922 changed the Russian empire into a new nation, called

◄ *Lenin and Stalin in rare agreement.*

the Union of Soviet Socialist Republics (USSR).

- **Joseph Stalin** (1879-1953) became dictator of the USSR after Lenin died in 1924, and remained so until he himself died, in 1953.

- **Stalin** was from Georgia and his real name was Joseph Vissarionovich Dzhugashvili.

- **Stalin used terror** to wipe out opposition and ensure the Revolution survived. Russians lived in fear of the secret police NKVD (later the KGB), led by Beria, and millions went to their deaths in the *Stalags* (prison camps).

- **Millions of Russian peasants** starved in the 1930s as Stalin forced through government control of farms.

- **Stalin's** industrial programme transformed the USSR into one of the world's great industrial and military powers.

Hitler

- **Adolf Hilter** (1889-1945) was the dictator who turned Germany into a war machine that started World War **2** and murdered 6 million Jews in the Holocaust.

- **Hitler** was born in Braunau, Austria. A failed artist, he painted postcards before joining the German army in World War 1.

- **Hitler** was so angry at the terms ending World War 1 that he joined the National Socialist (Nazi) party, becoming its leader.

▲*Hitler was a mesmerizing speaker, with the power to get the whole audience at his huge rallies shouting his praise.*

- **In 1923,** Hitler was put in prison after a failed Nazi coup, and there he wrote *Mein Kampf* ('My Struggle').

- *Mein Kampf* says Germany's problems were caused by Jews and communists and that it needed a strong *führer* (leader).

- **As the Depression** hit Germany in the early 1930s, Hitler's ideas gained support. In the 1933 elections, the Nazis got 37% of the vote and President Hindenburg asked Hitler to become chancellor (chief minister).

- **The Nazis** gained control of the *Gestapo* (police) and used them to wipe out all opposition. When Hindenburg died in 1934, Hitler made himself führer.

- **Hitler** built up Germany's army, rigidly organized all workers and sent millions of Jews to concentration camps.

- **In 1938,** Hitler invaded Austria, then in 1939 Czechoslovkia and Poland too, and so began World War 2.

- **Finally,** as Germany faced defeat in 1945, he married his mistress Eva Braun on 29 April, in their bomb shelter in Berlin. They shot themselves the next day.

The Spanish Civil War

◀ A recruiting poster for the fascist Falange party.

- **In the 1920s**, a weak economy and political unrest led General de Rivera to run Spain as dictator, alongside King Alfonso XIII.

- **In 1930**, the army drove Rivera out. In 1931, a popular vote for a republic persuaded Alfonso to leave Spain.

- **Spain** was split. On the Left were socialists, communists and ordinary people who supported the republic. On the right were wealthy landowners, army officers, the Catholic Church, and the fascist Falange party, who wanted the king back.

- **Complicating the picture** were Catalonians and Basques, who wanted to break away from Spain.

- **In February 1936**, elections put the Popular Front, formed by all the left-wing groups, in power.

- **In July 1936**, a wave of army revolts started in Morocco and threatened to topple the Popular Front. The Popular Front supporters armed themselves and a bitter civil war began, with terrible atrocities on both sides.

- **The forces of the Right** were called the Nationalists and were led by General Franco. They were supported by fascist (very right-wing) Germany and Italy.

- **The forces of the Left** were called the Republicans or Loyalists and were supported by Soviet Russia. Liberals from other countries, like the writer Laurie Lee, formed an International Brigade to fight for the Loyalists.

- **At first**, Loyalists held the northeast and the big cities, but they gradually fell back. In March 1936, Franco's forces captured Madrid, the last Loyalist stronghold.

- **Franco** was dictator of Spain until he died in 1975.

The Long March

- **In 1912**, the last Chinese emperor, six-year-old Pu-Yi, gave up his throne in the face of rebellion, and China became a republic, led by Sun Yat-sen.

- **When Sun** died, in 1925, leadership of his *Kuomintang* (Nationalist) party fell to Chiang Kai-shek, who allied with Communists to defeat warlords in the north.

- **In 1927**, Chiang Kai-shek turned on the Communists and forced their leaders to flee to the Jiangxi hills as he took control in Beijing.

- **By 1931**, the Communists had regrouped enough to set up a rival government in the south, called the Jiangxi soviet.

▶ The heroic Long March of the Red Army – to escape the Nationalists – became the stuff of Chinese legend.

✚ Red Army victories

✚ Turning points

- **In 1934**, Chiang Kai-shek launched a massive attack on the Communist Red Army, forcing them to begin their famous Long March to the north to escape.

- **On the Long March**, the Red Army wound 10,000 km through the mountains, covering up to 100 km a day, until they reached Shaanxi in the north a year later.

- **Almost 95,000** of the 100,000 who set out on the Long March died of cold and hunger on the way. But, crucially, the Red Army survived.

- **During the March**, Mao Zedong became the Red Army leader.

- **Chiang** was forced to join with Mao to fight Japan in World War 2, and Mao built up Red Army forces.

- **After the war**, Mao drove the weakened Kuomintang out and took control. Chiang fled to Taiwan.

World War 2

▲▶ In the crucial Battle of Britain, in 1940, heavily outnumbered British fighter planes eventually put a stop to massive German bombing raids on London and other English cities.

▶ Winston Churchill (1874-1965) was the British prime minister whose courage and inspiring speeches helped the British withstand the German threat.

'Never in the field of human conflict have so many owed so much to so few' – Churchill on the British fighter pilots.

> ★ STAR FACT ★
> The key to the early German successes was the Blitzkrieg ('lightning war') – a stunningly rapid attack with tanks and aeroplanes.

- **World War 2** (1939-45) was the most terrible war ever fought. It not only killed 17 million soldiers – compared to 10 million in World War 1 – but also twice as many civilians, through starvation, bombings and massacres.

- **It was the first** truly global war – fought on the plains of Europe, in the jungles of Southeast Asia, on the deserts of Africa, among the islands of the Pacific, on (and under) the Atlantic Ocean, and in many other places.

- **It began** when Hitler's Germany invaded Poland on 1 September 1939. Great Britain thought the USSR would defend Poland but Hitler and Stalin made a pact. As Germany invaded Poland from the west, the USSR invaded from the east.

- **After a lull**, or 'Phoney War', in May–June 1940, the Germans quickly overran Norway and Denmark, then

▶ There were two main areas of war. 1. Europe, where Britain and the USSR, and later the USA, were fighting Germany and Italy. 2. The Pacific and SE Asia, where the US and Britain were fighting Japan.

Luxembourg, the Netherlands, Belgium and France.

- **The British army** was trapped by the Channel coast, but the Germans held back, and 338,000 British troops got away from Dunkirk, France, on an armada of little boats.

- **By August 1940,** Italy joined the war on the German side, and Germany launched air raids on England to prepare for an invasion. This was the Battle of Britain (above).

- **Fearing the USSR** would turn against him, Hitler launched a sudden invasion of the USSR on 22 June 1941. The USA joined the war when Japan bombed its fleet without warning in Pearl Harbor, Hawaii, on 7 Dec 1941.

- **Germany, Italy, Japan** and six other nations joined forces as the 'Axis'. Britain, the USA, USSR, China and 50 other nations were together called the Allies. In 1942, the Allies halted the Axis in Africa, invading Italy in 1943 and France in 1944. In 1945, the Allies drove into Germany from east and west. Germany surrendered on 7 May 1945. The terrible Pacific conflict ended when the USA dropped atom bombs on the Japanese cities Hiroshima and Nagasaki. Japan surrendered on 2 Sept 1945.

- **As the Allies** moved into Germany, they found the horror of Nazi death camps like Auschwitz and Buchenwald, where millions of Jews and others had been slaughtered by starvation and in gas chambers.

Battle of Britain
Stalingrad
North Atlantic
El Alamein
Iwo Jima
Burma
Philippines

❋ Crucial campaigns
➡ Early Axis advances, 1939-41
➡ Allied advances in the Pacific, 1943-45

India

- **Indian discontent** with British rule began to boil after the British killed 400 protestors at Amritsar, in 1920.

- **In 1920**, Mahatma Gandhi became the leader of a movement demanding independence for India.

- **Gandhi** led a series of non-violent protests against the British, such as boycotting British goods and refusing to pay taxes. He gained millions of supporters.

- **In 1930,** Gandhi marched to the sea to make salt from seawater in protest against a tax on salt.

- **In 1935,** the British gave India a new constitution that allowed Indians more power. For the Muslims, however, led by Mohammed Ali Jinnah, this was not enough.

- **Jinnah** demanded a new country for Muslims called Pakistan, separate from the Hindus.

- **In World War 2,** Indians said they would only fight on the British side if they were given independence.

- **In 1942,** Gandhi launched his 'Quit India' campaign to get rid of the British, who then jailed Indian leaders.

▲ *The Indian government building in Delhi.*

- **In 1946,** Britain offered independence to all of India, but Muslims did not want to live under a Hindu majority and terrible riots broke out in Calcutta.

- **Indian and British** leaders agreed to partition (split) India and Pakistan. Pakistan became independent on 14 August 1947, India the next day. 7.5 million Muslims immediately fled to Pakistan and 10 million Hindus to India.

Mao

▶ *Mao Zedong was a man of vision – a brilliant general, a cunning politician, and a poet and philosopher. But he was also ruthlessly cruel.*

- **Mao Zedong** (1893-1976) led China's struggle towards communism and was China's leader for 27 years.

- **Mao was** born in 1893 to a poor peasant family in Shaoshan in Hunan.

- **In 1921,** he and 11 others formed the Chinese Communist Party. As support grew, Mao taught peasants guerilla tactics. He led the Red Army on the Long March.

- **Mao** led the communist takeover of China in 1949 and then ruled China as chairman of the republic. Chinese people hoped communism would end poverty and oppression. 'We have stood up,' Mao said.

- **Mao** spurred peasants to turf out landlords and work together on collective farms. Peasants who had starved in the war ate again. Healthcare and education improved.

- **Mao's** ideas were stated in a little red book – *The Thoughts of Chairman Mao* – learned by heart by Chinese children.

- **In 1957**, Mao's 'Great Leap Forward' forced his people to work on communes to develop farming and industry. The upheaval brought famine and economic disaster.

- **In 1959,** Mao retired as chairman, but stayed in control.

- **In 1966,** Mao launched a 'Cultural Revolution' to purge China of corrupting foreign ideas. Led by Mao's wife Jiang Qing and friends (the Gang of Four) Mao's enemies were killed and scholars were tortured and imprisoned.

- **Mao died** in 1976 and the Gang of Four were driven out.

Gandhi

◀ Gandhi always dressed with extreme simplicity, wearing just a plain robe and shorts, his feet bare or in sandals.

- **Mohandas Gandhi** (1869-1948) was the inspirational leader who led India's fight for independence in a remarkable campaign of non-violent protest.

- **Gandhi** is often called *Mahatma*, which means 'Great Soul'. He believed truth could only be known through tolerance and concern for others.

- **He was born** in Probander in India. At 13, he married a girl of 13 called Kasturba. They later had four children. At 14, he went to study law in London.

- **Gandhi** went to work as a lawyer in South Africa in 1893, but soon after arriving was thrown out of a railway carriage because of the colour of his skin. He then stayed in South Africa for 21 years to fight for Indian rights.

- **Gandhi** emphasized non-violent protest. By imposing hardship on himself and showing no anger or hatred, he believed he could persuade his opponents he was right. This method of action was called *Satyagraha*.

- **Gandhi** returned to India in 1915, and after the Amritsar massacre led India's fight for independence.

- **In 1920,** Gandhi began a programme of hand-spinning and weaving that he believed would give Indians economic independence, so challenging the British.

- **Gandhi** was jailed again and again for his protests, both in South Africa and India, and spent seven years in jail.

- **Gandhi** was assassinated on 30 January 1948, by a Hindu who hated his tolerance of Muslims and others.

> ★ **STAR FACT** ★
> In 1948, Gandhi persuaded Hindus and Muslims to stop fighting by going on a fast.

Israel

- **In the 1920s,** Palestine was under British rule, and the British encouraged Jews to settle there.

- **In the aftermath** of the Holocaust, when Hitler killed six million Jews, most countries supported the idea of a homeland where Jews would be free from persecution.

- **In 1948,** the United Nations split Palestine between Arabs and Jews. Arabs saw this as a theft of Arab land.

- **Arabs immediately** invaded Israel (Jewish Palestine), but were defeated. Israel took over all of Palestine except the Gaza strip (to Egypt) and the West Bank (to Jordan).

- **In 1956-57,** Arab Egypt took control of the Suez Canal.

- **In 1967,** Egypt closed the Gulf of Aqaba, Israel's only way to the Red Sea. Israel declared war on the Arab states.

- **Israel** won the war in just six days, and calls it the 'Six Day War'. Arabs call it the June War. Afterwards, Israel controlled Sinai, the Gaza strip and the West Bank.

- **In 1973,** Egypt attacked the Israelis in Sinai, starting the Yom Kippur War. With US help, the Israelis repulsed them.

- **By the Camp David Accords** of 1978, Egypt recognized Israel's right to exist and Israel returned Sinai to Egypt. US president Jimmy Carter set up the agreement.

- **The PLO,** led by Yasser Arafat, began to fight for Palestinian independence after the Six Day War. Fighting and negotiation continue to this day.

▼ *An Israeli tank taking part in 1967's Six Day War.*

The Cold War

▲ For many, the tearing down of the Berlin Wall, in 1989, marked the end of the Cold War. Berliners had a huge party on the ruins.

- **The Cold War** was the rivalry between communist and non-communist countries after World War 2 – between the USSR and USA in particular.

- **It was called** the Cold War because the USSR and USA did not fight directly. But both supported countries that did – like the USA in Vietnam and the USSR in Korea.

- **The Iron Curtain** was the barrier between western Europe and communist eastern Europe.

- **The name Iron Curtain** was invented by German propagandist Goebbels and adopted by Churchill.

- **The Berlin Wall** dividing communist East Berlin from the West was a powerful Cold War symbol. Hundreds were shot trying to escape from the East over the wall.

- **The Cold War** was fought using both propaganda and art and by secret means such as spies and secret agents.

- **The USA and USSR** waged an arms race to build up nuclear bombs and missiles one step ahead of their rival.

- **Real war** loomed when US president Kennedy threatened the USSR as it tried to build missile bases on Cuba in 1962.

- **The Cold War** thawed after 1985, when Soviet leader Mikhail Gorbachev introduced reforms in the USSR and began to co-operate with the West.

- **In 1989,** the Berlin Wall came down. In 1989-90, many eastern European countries broke away from Soviet control.

Scandinavia

- **In 1397,** Sweden, Norway and Denmark had joined together as one kingdom to combat the threat of German influence.

- **In 1523,** a Swedish noble called Gustavus Vasa took Sweden out of the Union. Under Gustavus Adolphus (ruled 1611-1632), and later Charles XII (ruled 1697-1718), Sweden became a powerful nation in its own right, and gained possession of Finland.

- **After the Napoleonic Wars,** Sweden lost Finland, but gained Norway from Denmark, which had sided with the defeated France.

- **In the 1800s,** Norwegians began to revive national traditions – like the Viking language and 'Hardanger' fiddle music – and demand independence from Sweden. This was finally granted in September 1905.

◀ Copenhagen's most famous landmark is the 1913 statue of the Little Mermaid, from the famous tale by Danish 19th-century children's writer, Hans Christian Andersen.

- **In World War 2,** Norway tried to remain neutral, but Germany invaded.

- **The Germans** made a Norwegian who helped them, Vidkund Quisling, prime minister. *Quisling* is now a word for traitor.

- **Since 1932,** Sweden has been governed mostly by the socialist SDP, who have spread Sweden's high standard of living to all levels of society.

- **In 1966,** the National Insurance Act passed by Norway's *Storting* (parliament) gave Norwegians one of the world's best welfare systems.

- **In 1986,** Swedish PM Olof Palme was assassinated.

- **Sweden and Denmark** joined the European Union in the 1990s; Norwegians voted against joining in 1994.

Japan

▶ Emperor Hirohito (1901-89) was the first Japanese emperor to give up his god-like status, ruling after 1945 as a figurehead only.

- **In 1942**, Japanese conquests in World War 2 gave it a huge empire across SE Asia, but after they lost the decisive naval battle of Midway to the USA, the tide turned against Japan.

- **The final blow** for the Japanese was the devastating atomic bombs dropped on the cities of Hiroshima (6 August 1945) and Nagasaki (9 Aug).

- **The Japanese** surrendered to the USA on 14 August 1945.

- **The surrender** brought a foreign occupying force to Japan, led by US general, Douglas MacArthur.

- **MacArthur** drew up a new constitution for Japan. Under this, Emperor Hirohito lost all real power.

- **The Americans** shared out farmland, legalized unions and improved women's and children's rights.

- **The occupation force** left in 1952.

- **Led by the government,** Japan recovered from the ruin of the war and launched itself on an amazing industrial boom which turned Japan into the world's healthiest economy in barely 25 years.

- **Japanese** society changed as people moved to the cities and the young began to behave independently.

- **In the 1980s**, the government was rocked by corruption scandals. The economy suffered too, as exports declined, and the country experienced a crisis of confidence.

South Africa

- **In 1910**, four British colonies – Transvaal, Orange Free State, Cape Colony and Natal – joined to make the self-governing Union of South Africa.

- **White people** had almost complete power in the Union, and blacks had virtually no legal rights.

- **Gandhi** campaigned for Indian rights in South Africa and had limited success.

◀ Many blacks were tortured, imprisoned or killed in the long and bitter struggle against apartheid. 600 died here at Soweto in 1976.

- **When Gandhi** returned to India, black South Africans set up their own campaign in 1912 with the movement later called the ANC (African National Congress).

- **Afrikaners** – descended from the Dutch Boer people – began to fight for control. Their National Party made headway and in 1948 came to power. It enacted 'apartheid' laws to keep all the races firmly apart.

- **The ANC** fought against apartheid – and especially against 'pass' laws that meant blacks had to carry passes.

- **In 1960**, police opened fire on protesting blacks at Sharpeville, killing 69. The government banned the ANC.

- **In the 1970s and 80s**, opposition to apartheid grew both in and outside South Africa, with many countries applying sanctions (trade restrictions).

- **In 1990**, President de Klerk released Nelson Mandela, an activist jailed since 1962, and repealed apartheid laws.

- **In 1994**, the ANC won the first open elections and Nelson Mandela became South Africa's first black president.

United Nations

- **In the aftermath** of World War 1, the great powers had set up a League of Nations – a forum for nations to come together, discuss world problems and so avoid war.

- **In 1942**, the Allies pledged to fight against the Axis powers with a statement called the Declaration by United Nations.

- **In 1944**, the same nations – including Britain, the USA, USSR and China – got together at Dumbarton Oaks in Washington DC to try and set up a peacekeeping organization.

- **The key to the** Dumbarton Oaks plan was a Security Council in which Britain, the USA, USSR and China would be permanent members.

- **In February 1945**, US president Roosevelt, British PM Churchill and Soviet leader Stalin met at Yalta in the Crimea and announced that a UN conference would meet in San Francisco. The three introduced the idea of them having a special veto (right to reject UN measures).

◄ The UN flag flies over its permanent headquarters in New York.

- **50 nations** met at San Francisco in April 1945 to draw up the Charter for the United Nations.

- **The Big Three** – Britain, the USA and USSR – gave themselves veto power over the Security Council, but the smaller nations gave the UN a General Assembly to help make it a truly global organization.

- **The UN Charter** came into effect on 24 October 1945.

- **In 1971**, the UN expelled Taiwan and admitted Communist China instead.

- **In recent years**, the UN peacekeeping force has been involved in keeping the peace in many places, including Somalia, Rwanda, Kosovo, Sierra Leone and E.Timor.

Vietnam

- **From 1883**, Vietnam, along with Cambodia and Laos, was ruled by France as French Indochina or *Indochine*.

- **As Germany** invaded France in World War 2, Japan took over Vietnam.

- **When Japan** lost, in 1945, Vietnamese communists – the Vietminh – led by Ho Chi Minh, took over Vietnam.

- **British and Chinese** troops reclaimed Vietnam for the French, but the Vietminh fought back. The French set up a State of Vietnam under Bao Dai to oppose the Vietminh.

- **In 1954**, the warring parties agreed to split Vietnam into the North under Ho Chi Minh and South under Bao Dai.

- **The Vietminh-backed** Viet Cong started a rebellion in the South. In 1965, the USA began to bomb North Vietnam, while the USSR and China gave them arms.

▲ US helicopters proved highly effective in the Vietnam jungles.

- **As fighting escalated**, Americans began to protest against US involvement and in 1973, the US withdrew.

- **In 1975**, the Viet Cong captured Saigon, the capital of the South, and the next year united North and South.

- **One million** Vietnamese left as refugees, but by 2000, Vietnam was developing quietly and some returned.

★ STAR FACT ★
The Vietnamese war was the first war that was widely televised as it happened.

Iraq and Iran

- **Iran** used to be called Persia, which, 2,500 years ago, ruled over one of the great ancient empires.

- **The last shah** (king) of Iran, Muhammad Reza, although backed by the USA, was forced to flee the country in 1979 by Islamic extremists, led by the *ayatollah* (priest), Khomeini.

- **Iraq** used to be called Mesopotamia and was part of the Turkish Ottoman Empire until 1921 when it became a British possession.

- **In 1930**, Britain promised Iraq independence. But British

IRAQ · Baghdad · Teheran · IRAN · Shatt al-Arab · Kuwait · Persian Gulf

◄ *Iran and Iraq have a long and disputed common border.*

influence remained crucial until the last king, Faisal I, was killed and Iraq became a republic.

- **After years** of wrangling, Saddam Hussein became Iraqi president.

- **Saddam Hussein** was worried by the unsettling effects of the Islamic revolution in Iran and was also eager to regain some disputed territory.

- **In September 1980**, Iraq invaded Iran to begin the eight-year-long Iran-Iraq War.

- **The vicious war** devastated both countries and killed 1.5 million people. Iraq launched deadly bombing raids and Iran replied with missile attacks on Baghdad.

- **In 1988**, careful negotiations by the UN leader Perez de Cuéllar arranged a peace settlement.

> ★ **STAR FACT** ★
> No war has ever used chemical weapons more devastatingly than the Iran-Iraq War.

The break-up of Russia

- **After Stalin died**, in 1953, many people were released from the Siberian prison camps, but the USSR, under its new leader Khrushchev, stayed restrictive and secretive.

- **The KGB** was a secret police force set up under Yuri Andropov. It dealt harshly with anyone who did not toe the communist line.

- **In the 1980s**, cracks began to appear in the communist machine.

- **In 1985**, Mikhail Gorbachev became Soviet leader and introduced policies of *perestroika* (economic reform), *glasnost* (government openness) and *demokratizatsiya* (increased democracy).

- **Gorbachev** also made cuts in army spending and improved relationships with the West.

◄ *Mikhail Gorbachev.*

- **In 1989**, a McDonalds restaurant opened in Moscow.

- **As people** in the USSR gained freedom, so people in communist eastern Europe demanded freedom. New democratic governments were elected in Hungary, Poland, Czechoslovakia, Romania and Bulgaria.

- **The republics** within the USSR demanded independence too, and in 1991 the USSR was dissolved and replaced by a Commonwealth of Independent States (CIS).

- **Gorbachev's reforms** angered Communist Party leaders, who staged a coup and imprisoned Gorbachev, but he was freed and the coup was brought down by Boris Yeltsin, who became Russia's first president.

- **Under Yeltsin**, the state industries of the Soviet era were gradually broken up and Russia seemed to be moving towards Western-style capitalism. But the collapse of the Communist Party structure led to chaos, lawlessness and economic problems. In 2000, the Russians elected Vladimir Putin as president, a strong leader who they hoped would see them out of the crisis.

The European Union

◄ The European Commission building in Strasbourg. The Parliament is in Brussels. The Court of Justice is in Luxembourg.

- **The European Union** is an organization of 15 European countries, including France, Germany and the UK.

- **After World War 2** ended in 1945, Jean Monet promoted the idea of uniting Europe economically and politically.

- **In 1951**, six countries formed the European Coal and Steel Community (ECSC), to trade in coal and steel.

- **The success of the ECSC** led the member countries to break down all trade barriers between them as part of the European Community (EC), in 1967.

- **1973-81:** six new countries join the EC, including the UK.

- **In 1992**, the 12 EC members signed a treaty at Maastricht in the Netherlands to form the European Union (EU).

- **The EU** added cooperation on justice and police matters and cooperation in foreign and security affairs to the economic links of the EC. These three links are called the 'Three Pillars' of the EU.

- **The EU** has four governing bodies: the Commission, Council of Ministers, Court of Justice and Parliament. The 17 Commissioners submit laws for the Council to make and put into effect. Parliament has very limited powers but is gaining more each year.

- **In 1999**, the EU launched the Euro, which is intended to become a single European currency.

> **! NEWS FLASH !**
> Poland, Hungary, the Czech Republic, Estonia and Cyprus will soon join the EU.

Latin America

- **In the 1950s**, many Latin American governments sought to break their dependence on single farm products such as sugar and beef through major industrialization programmes.

- **'Populist' alliances** between workers and industrialists came to the fore.

- **In Argentina**, Juan Perón came to power and tried to build up industry at the expense of agriculture.

- **Landowners** suffering from the emphasis on industry began to form alliances with the army. Army coups took place in Argentina (1955), Brazil (1964) and Chile (1973).

- **Many** of the military regimes were secretly backed by foreign powers such as the USA.

▲ Che Guevara became a hero to political activists throughout the world.

- **In the 1960s**, some Latin American groups resorted to guerilla warfare to bring down the military dictatorships.

- **In 1959**, an Argentinian communist called Che Guevara helped overthrow the dictator of Cuba and bring Fidel Castro to power.

- **In 1965**, Che Guevara was killed leading a guerilla band trying to overthrow the dictator of Bolivia.

- **Under the dictators**, opposition was suppressed and many people were tortured, imprisoned or 'disappeared', as 20,000 did in Argentina.

- **In the 1980s and 90s**, economic failure brought down most Latin American dictators, including Pinochet in Chile (1990) and Galtieri in Argentina (1983).

INDEX

ACKNOWLEDGEMENTS

Artists: Vanessa Card, Chris Forsey, Mike Foster, Terry Gabbey/AFA, Richard Hook/Linden Artists, John James/Temple Rogers, Roger Kent/Illustration, Terry Riley, Rob Sheffield, Mike Taylor/SGA, Mike White, John Woodcock

The publishers thank the following sources for the use of their photographs:
Page 8 (B/C) Illustrated London News; Page 13 (B/C) Lowell Georgia/CORBIS; Page 19 (B/R) Vanni Archive/CORBIS; Page 21 (B/R) LindsayHebberd/CORBIS; Page 22 (B/L) Michael Nicholson/CORBIS; Page 42 (T/L) Staffan Widstrand/CORBIS; Page 49 (B/R) Christel Gerstenberg/CORBIS; Page 51 (B/R) Bojan Brecelj/CORBIS; Page 59 (T/R) Aachen Tourist Board Page 67 (T/R) Gianni Dagli Orti/CORBIS; Page 67 (B/R) Bettmann/CORBIS; Page 69 (T/R) Burstein Collection/CORBIS; Page 72 (T/L) Angelo Hornak/CORBIS; Page 72 (B/C) Michael Maslan Historic Photographs/CORBIS; Page 77 (T/R) Yann Arthus-Bertrand/CORBIS; Page 77 (B/C) Yann Arthus-Bertrand/CORBIS; Page 79 (C/B) Gianni Dagli Orti/CORBIS; Page 81 CORBIS; Page 82 (B/L) Dave G. Houser/CORBIS; Page 86 (T/R) Bettmann/CORBIS; Page 89 (B/R) Macduff Everton/CORBIS; Page 91 (B/R) Gianni Dagli Orti/CORBIS; Page 94 (B/R) Reuters NewMedia Inc./CORBIS; Page 98 (T/R) Hulton-Deutsch Collection/CORBIS; Page 100 (T/C) Archivo Iconografico/CORBIS; Page 105 (T/C) Bettmann/CORBIS; Page 107 (T/C) Historical Picture Archive/CORBIS; Page 108 (T/L) Sean Sexton Collection/CORBIS; Page 109 (B/R) Bettmann/CORBIS; Page 111 (T/C) Historical Picture Archive/CORBIS; Page 112 (T/L) CORBIS; Page 114 (T/L) Museum of Flight/CORBIS; Page 115 (T/R) Angelo Hornak/CORBIS; Page 116 (B/L) Vittoriano Rastelli/CORBIS; Page 118 (B/L) Hulton-Deutsch Collection/CORBIS; Page 119 (B/R) Bettmann/CORBIS; Page 121 (B/R) Tom Bean/CORBIS.

All other photographs are from MKP Archives.

Every effort has been made to obtain permission for copyright material reproduced within this compilation. If however, the publishers have inadvertently made any error or omission, they would be grateful for notification and happy to correct it in any future reprints.